The
TRUE
You

An Awakening and Happiness Manual
By
Erica Rock

Truths About You 11

As You Read, You Will Open to Divine Grace 13

As Your True Self Begins to Unfold... 15

How to Work with this Book.. 19

Expect Changes in Your Life 20

More About Grace Blessings 22

Exposure to Grace Will Give You 23
Direct Experience of The Divine. 23
Can Grace Blessings Help with Physical Healing? 24

Working with Your Vibration 25

How to Change Your Vibration...................................... 26

The Heart Check-in.. 27

All You Need Is YOU! 28

Setting Mile-Markers for Reflection 30

Life Should Always Be Easy!...................................... 33

Shifting Your Consciousness...................................... 35

The Formula for Success Is *Let Go and Let God* 36

Using Your Free Will 37

Moving into Acceptance, ... 38

When Not to Simply Accept.. 40

Let Go and Let God 42

Prayer as a Tool for "Letting Go and Letting God" 44

Claim the "I AM" 46

"I AM" Statements Create a Space of Being........................ 48

Letting Go: Learning the Art of Prostration 49

Step by Step, the Process of Prostrating: 49

Release Your Expectations of Results 51

Sometimes, the Guidance is *"Wait and See."* 51

More Personal Experience 52

When You Should Prostrate 53

An Example from My Life 54

Another Example 55

Are You Ready for Your First Grace Blessing? 57

How The Blessings Are Shared 60

Awareness of the False Self 62

This Can Be So Easy! 64

Of Lisa and Laughter 66

The Art of Appreciation 67

The Importance of Feeling 69

About Empathic Sensitivity 70

Get Real with How You Feel, That's the Deal! 71

Grandma's Real World Example 72

Gifts in Everything We Experience 73

We Choose Our Perspective, Even in Pain 75

Let's Look at this Idea From a More Global Perspective... 76

Working with Relationships 77

Changing the Focus 78

About Your Worthiness 80

You Are Worthy! 82

Befriend Your Mind 84

Focus on YOU First 86

Where There Is Light, There Cannot Be Darkness 87

More Illumination for You: 89

Mastery of Mind and Emotions 90
   Tips for Feeling Into Your Emotions 91

How to "Feel into a Feeling" 93

Your Next Grace Blessing 95

Drop the Drama 97
   Remember How You Were When You Were Little 97

Resolving Conflict 99
   What to Do when You're Upset 100
   Why I Stress Relationships 100

Misperceptions Cause Suffering 102
   Seek to Understand the Behavior of Others 103

About Judgment 104
   A Real Life Example of Judgment, Stories and Perception 104

Setting Relationships Right: Peacemaking & Forgiveness 106

About "The Gift of Life Prayers" 107
   Hints and Tips 107

"Healing Is a Feeling" by Howard Wills 110
   "Practice To Natural Healing" By Howard Wills: 112
   The Roadmap 114
   Ancestral Prayer 115
   Forgiveness Affirmation 116
   Prayer of Personal Forgiveness 117
   Prayer of Complete Personal Forgiveness 119
   Prayer of Generational Forgiveness 122
   Prayer for All Races, All Nations, All Humanity, The Earth, and All Life 124
   Prayer of Complete Healing for all Relationships 125
   Prayer of Complete Personal Healing 127
   Prayer of Thanks 129

The Prayer of Bounty.. 130
The Prayer of Freedom... 131
The Forgiveness List: An Exercise in Freeing Yourself. 132
Create a God that Works for You 135
Building a Divine Relationship 136
Deepening the Relationship Within 137
The Mind Likes to Question 139
Another Question of the Mind 140
How Can It Get Any Better Than This? 141
You Can Shift Reality in the Blink of an Eye...................... 143
A Real Life Example 145
Separated From God... 146
From Drama to Ease 148
Meditating.. 149
A Practice of Appreciation....................................... 150
Physical Illness 152
The Importance of Conscious Breathing 155
Circular Breathing... 156
Your Mind Is Trying to Help You 158
A client recently gave another example of this in action: 158
My Own Unfolding 159
Celebrate One Another's Victories 161
Acts of Kindness.. 163
What is Enlightenment? 165
Your Feelings are Your Map 167
Practice Not Naming Your Emotions............................. 168
Get Acquainted with Your Feelings 169
Slow and Steady, One Step at a Time 171

The Power is Always Within You! 173

Anger as a Gateway to Reclaiming Power 174

Divine Grace Does Not Override Free Will 175

Letting Go of Beliefs that No Longer Serve You 176

Create a Give It Over to God List 177

What If This Still Isn't Working? 178

Remove ALL Limitations from Yourself and Be Happy
NOW! 180

The Power of Focus... 182

What Is Holding Up Your Happiness? 183

Happiness Will Begin to Feel Normal........................... 185

Every Single Day.. 187

Your Next Grace Blessing 188

Sleep On It, Dream On It!....................................... 189

   The Deliberate Art of Daydreaming........................... 190

How Can You Help the People Around You?..................... 191

Do You Feel Like You're on a Roller Coaster?................... 193

Create a "God Box".. 194

With Love, From Erica Rock..................................... 195

Appendix: Further Support & Grace Blessings Resources 199

Many paths lead to Awakening, the path
of grace is the path of no work, the deep of
endless spiritual seeking, healing, fixing, clear your
"issues" can be over, all it takes is for you
to say "yes" and commit.

IMPORTANT PLEASE READ!

The artwork, created by Sven Geier, contained in this book is infused with Divine Grace to initiate your enlightenment process. The artwork you find here is in black and white. The black and white picture in no way affects the strength or power of the blessing you are receiving. However, Erica has a treat for you. Since you bought this book, she wishes to gift you the e-book version for FREE, which has all the artwork in color. The artwork is so very beautiful to gaze at in all its vibrant glory, so be sure to go to http://shop.ericarock.com/registerthetrueyou and register to receive your FREE full color e-book

Truths About You

You are alive on this planet at one of the greatest times in history, here to experience the infinite potential inside you.

You are here to play a significant role in the evolution of consciousness, on this great Earth. You've come to participate in the unification of humanity.

You have the support, love and light of Divine Grace to help achieve this potential, to achieve YOUR potential.

YOU are needed, NOW.
Your light is needed, NOW.
So I ask you to shine brightly.

And I ask you to say Yes.

Say Yes to life.
Say Yes to why you are here, why you are here now.
Say Yes to why you have incarnated.
Say Yes to your gifts, abilities and talents.
Say Yes to the unfolding of our new reality and new Earth.

I know who you are with all of my love and heart. I know why you are here, and I know the magnificence and brilliance of what you carry inside of you. Say Yes and add your light, your spark, to the evolution of our species.

Are You ready to awaken
to the Majesty
of the Light and Love
that You truly are?

The time for awakening is this moment.

Never before has enlightenment and a return to wholeness been so readily accessible to *All*.

Through this book, I offer you an invitation to join me (and countless others) in an unending, endless flowering of our authentic selves. It is an experience free of suffering, free of mental chatter, free of pain of all types and kinds. It is freedom; pure, easy, simple…free.

As You Read, You Will Open to Divine Grace

The artwork and words you'll find here are infused with Divine Energy, energy that will initiate your awakening process and enlightenment. This process is unique to each individual, so do not try and compare your journey to mine, or to anyone else's. Your path is exquisitely unique, custom tailored for you, and my wish, my goal, for you is that you may have your own journey, your own experience of Grace.

Enlightenment is not something you'll understand with your mind, it is something you'll understand with your heart. Sometimes, we try to gather more knowledge and information, hoping to understand more clearly, but more information can actually confuse you. That's because of the vast difference between mind knowing and direct experience of life.

Most of what we believe has been told to us; we haven't experienced it personally. What most people think of as truth in spirituality isn't something they've lived through, but something they've been taught. Yet, the only way you can be sure of something is if you have tangibly experienced it yourself, and no conversation, workshop, seminar or book about spirituality can substitute for the experience.

So don't look for similarities to a teacher's path to validate your journey... your experience of the journey is its own validation. You only have your mind-knowing of anyone else's journey, and not the experience, so there is no comparison. The same is true of anyone who would judge your path - they do not know the experience, so they cannot know or compare your journey to theirs.

Have your own journey. Don't expect it to be like anyone else's. No one individual's path is more important or more valid than another's. I do not know what your journey will look like; it is yours and yours alone to experience.

As Your True Self Begins to Unfold...

You will begin to experience the Divine within and around you in ways beyond words, ways beyond explanation. If you already have a strong connection with the Divine, you may find that connection opening further, and deepening. Either way, I'd like you to ask yourself: "How would I like my life to look? How do I wish to feel?"

This book will help you attain your heart's true desires with ease, elegance and best of all Grace. As you read, you'll find many simple, effective tools to help you use your mind effectively, and exercise your freewill wisely.

I've included every useful tool from my personal toolbox. Each one has been personally used by me many times; I continue to use them because they work and work well. I've shared them with countless people all over the globe, who've also found that they work. These tools are intended to make the unfolding of your authentic self as delicious (even decadent!) as possible. I'm delighted to offer them, and I look forward to hearing your success stories and personal triumphs as you progress.

I probably could have summed up the entire process of awakening in three or four sentences, but the mind would have difficulty with that.

It is too simple.

But here is the wisdom and truth I know in my heart, the key to everything you need for eternal happiness:

Look upon everything in this world not with your eyes, but with your heart. Peace and quiet are your home; let peace be still within you.

Thrive in silence, listen in silence to the still soft voice that comes from the depth of your body and soul. All of the answers you seek are there, and this voice lives within us all.
The Grace that you find here will help you reach the stillness, the softness, the inner peace.

It is a flame, a spark that is within all of us and unifies us all.

Because that flame dwells within me, I am a spark, here to light the flame that dwells within you. You, in turn, are a spark, and once lit, you too will light the sparks of those around you. On it will go until all of our sparks are illuminated, burning with the brightness of a million suns.

Grace itself will do most of the work for you; all you need to do is to let go, and let it in. Do not *try* to let it in, just open yourself, open to it and allow it to awaken you to the True You.

Why I Wrote "The TRUE You"

For thousands of years, humanity has been harming itself, other life forms and even Mother Earth with our greed, violence, competitiveness, pollution, hatred, jealousy, envy, and non-consciousness.

It's time for humanity to wake up. It's time for us to take responsibility for all of our thoughts, words and actions, time to grow into the potential of who we are: a reflection and embodiment of the Divine.

We are the children of the Divine. As we accept this truth, we awaken to our authentic selves on personal, family, global and universal levels, and we shift into higher levels of consciousness. As we take full responsibility for our health, the health of other life forms, and the health of our planet, we become the stewards of the earth that we came here to be, living fully and freely on a peaceful Earth, returning to the Garden of Eden.

I want this book to help in that process. It's been writing itself through me, revealing itself bit by bit for many years. During this process, I've chosen not to have many "teachers" in human form, and was guided early on to NOT read many spiritual or self-help books.

Instead, I've learned directly by studying life, listening to the "still, soft voice", and by being aware and paying close attention to the world around and within me. As I've written and learned, I've spent a great deal of time in silence, communing only with the Divine Presence. Holding the intention to have all illusion lifted and Truth revealed, wanting to be free, live free and be liberated, I opened to Divine Grace, and in return, Divine Grace radically transformed my life.

As part of that transformation, I was initiated to give Grace Blessings to others. Now I assist people in remembering who they are and opening to Grace as I did; writing and publishing this book is part of that process, a way of reaching more people and accelerating the process of Global Awakening.

How to Work with this Book

The first time you go over this material, please read it in order, from beginning to end; it's arranged as it is for a reason. Read at a comfortable speed, without pushing yourself or rushing to finish; everyone absorbs the messages and energy in their own time. Listen to your own inner voice, let it guide your progress. The energy contained within this book can cause radical shifts in your life, so it's important to let the change move at its own pace.

The material is punctuated with Grace Blessings, a transfer of Divine Energy. To receive a Blessing, read the suggestions attached to it, then contemplate and gaze at the artwork for a few minutes. Each piece of artwork in this book has been infused with these Blessings; they are the primary vehicles for the energy that you'll receive as you work through the material. Make it a practice to engage the lessons and the energy in your day to day life.

I'll explain more about Grace Blessings later on in the book. For now, just understand that they are agents of change. Each one holds a positive, powerful experience for you!

Expect Changes in Your Life

As you wake up and begin to live as your authentic self, you'll find that your creativity flowers, inspiration abounds, and synchronicities become regular occurrences. Life will simply seem easier, more joyful. People, events and opportunities seem to show up out of nowhere, benefiting everyone around you. You may begin to feel that everything you touch turns to gold, and that the universe tilts for you - because it does!

Awakened, you'll begin (maybe for the first time ever!) to really live your life, moment by moment in the present. You'll find yourself captivated by living fully, completely and consciously in the now. In the now, worries over the past and future lose their hold.

As you awaken to the True You, you'll find yourself more balanced in life. Very little will be able to knock you off your center, and when it does happen, it won't be for long. Global events, the economy, death, breakups, divorce and other troubles will lose their impact. You will reclaim all of your power, knowing who you truly are and living your large, glorious radiant self right here on earth, having a joyous life. You will never give your power away to anyone or anything ever again.

When you see the world through your authentic self, you will see through the eyes of Truth, the eyes of the Divine. The Divine does not judge any event as good or bad, things just are as they are. You become in acceptance of "what is".

Grace is fully available to everyone all the time equally, just like air. Some people choose to breathe more deeply, therefore they take in more of what is readily available. Grace is the same way, it is always being offered. The Presence sends gifts and blessings daily but they are blocked by judgment, scorn, criticism, pride and other limiting attitudes.

Belief systems often can create blockages to the Grace that is pouring down.

This book will assist you in opening to Grace, to let it in, get out of the way and have fun in the process. Your old outdated belief systems, conditioning and patterns, all things that are not really you, will dissolve in time. If letting go of these conditioned patterns has been a challenge for you, rest assured, this book will help you with that.

Letting go is an art; like anything else you want to master, it takes practice. But this kind of practice won't feel like work! Bring a playful, joyful attitude to this material; all you have to do is relax, enjoy and experience.

More About Grace Blessings

Grace Blessings are difficult to explain, but simple to experience. They are transfers of Divine Energy; transmissions of light and intelligence that open you to the freely available Grace, Grace that has always been around you.

Sometimes, receiving a Grace Blessing is like a spiritual rotor rooter, forcing out everything that is not really you, cleaning out all of the sludge that is concealing the True You, opening the channels to the Source. There are likely all kinds of false beliefs, patterns, family and cultural conditioning that are blocking those channels - you may believe them, but they are not you, and so they limit your perceptions of Truth.

Grace Blessings dissolve and dissipate those blocks. As you receive the Blessings, your perception of yourself and of reality will radically transform; illusions will lift and you will see, feel and experience a greater Truth. Please know that even after your Blessings, this Truth may still seem to shift and change as you grow and progress. This is because what appears "true" at one level of consciousness can look different at another level of consciousness; there are always more illusions to shed, always a Greater Truth to be revealed.

As you discover these layers of Truth, you'll develop a complete acceptance of self, others and of all life. The freedom and liberation are beyond words. No matter what outer circumstances may look like you will have an unshakable peace and centeredness within. A fellow Blessings-giver said it like this, "You become free *with everything*, not necessarily free *of anything*." Challenging circumstance still happen, but they will seem less challenging because you are centered, balanced and *Blessed*.

Exposure to Grace Will Give You
Direct Experience of The Divine.

I will not ask you to have faith, ever. You don't need faith when you have direct experience. You will come to live as the Divine, fully awake and alive, creating, playing and living. You will get into the flow of life, the flow of Grace. Synchronicities become commonplace and life flows easily, almost magically; you may remember what this was like when you were a child.

As the saying goes, "Only like unto a little child will you enter into the kingdom of heaven." You are returning there once again, this time you will stay permanently.

This is what you have been searching for. The search is over, you have arrived.

Can Grace Blessings Help with Physical Healing?

People often ask if Grace Blessings can help with physical problems like disease and injury. I have seen people who have various diseases, aches and pains gain full resolution after receiving Grace Blessings, but I cannot claim or promise that Blessings will result in healing of medical issues, or any other specific situation. Each person, each situation, each resolution is different.

What I can tell you is that Albert Einstein once said, "A problem cannot be solved from the same consciousness in which it was created."

As people receive Grace Blessings, they shift levels of consciousness, sometimes very quickly. What seems true at one level of consciousness is not always true in another. Sometimes these shifts of perception and consciousness cause very significant changes, so significant that it's as if you've changed reality itself. *(Because you have!)*

In addition, since you are expanding consciousness, rapidly shifting and raising your personal vibration, you are less likely to be sick and hurting. So if you are seeking physical healing, let go of any expectations and be open to receive. Grace will give you exactly what you need and what you can allow in. There is more about physical healing later on in this book. Keep reading!

Working with Your Vibration

Everything in life is energy, and energy is always in motion, always vibrating. Even the Divine vibrates with energy! As human beings, we vibrate with energy, too. When our vibration is higher and faster, we feel better, happier, and in bliss - our life is more comfortable and whole. When our energy vibration is low, we feel sluggish, depressed, and negative, and we're more likely to struggle with strife, difficult attitudes and relationships.

To learn about the vibration that you're emitting, contemplate your body, your attitudes, your world and your life. Consider these questions:

- Are you healthy and well, or suffering from low energy and illness?

- Are you financially prosperous, or struggling to pay the bills?

- Are your relationships harmonious, or filled with discord?

- Does your social life leave you feeling fulfilled and excited, or empty, frustrated and alone?

Your experience of these life areas will vary with the frequency of your energy's vibration.

Blessedly, we have a great deal of control over our personal vibrations. Although it is not our fault that we are sick, troubled or alone, we can shift to a higher state, shifting our experience. We can raise our vibration so that even during difficult times, we'll remain in a higher, healthier state.

How to Change Your Vibration

To begin to shift your vibration to a better place, focus on a relationship you'd like to change. It can be a relationship with a person, place, or thing - even a relationship with yourself, or a part of yourself, like your health, your body or mind.

Holding that relationship in your mind, state your desired change in as clear and focused a way as possible. Now, ask yourself this question: "Am I moving toward this thing that I desire, or away from it?" The answer may come to you in a word, or a visual, or some other way - but it will always come in a way you can recognize.

When you move toward what you want, working in conjunction with your desire, the vibration of your energy is raised. But if you're moving away from your intent, working against your desire, your vibration will drop.

Understanding the relationship between desire and vibration will help you understand otherwise puzzling aspects of your situation. It can help you understand why your money situation is what it is, or help explain your relationship to your mate, job, or family. Consider what subtle changes you can make in your attitude or actions to bring yourself more in harmony with your desire, changes that will bring you more aligned with your goals. This will help raise your vibration to a more positive place of manifestation.

The Heart Check-in

Another practice to develop is a regular check-in with your heart, the soul of your emotions and purest desires. Before you take any action (including speaking), check in with your heart, see how it feels in response to what you are about to do or say. If the action doesn't feel good in your heart, don't take the action. If the words don't feel right in your heart, don't say those words.

That "not right" feeling means the action you're considering will move you further away from your desires. It will put you at odds with your intent, and lower your vibration. But if the proposed action makes your heart swell with joy, if it feels good and easy? Then you're on the right track! Do it, take action! If the words make you happy, if what you want to say makes your heart sing? Speak!

This practice will raise your vibration, and put you and your desires in harmony. It is a small and simple change you can make right now, a change you can make to raise your vibration, a change fully in your control.

Check in with your heart before you act or speak.

All You Need Is YOU!

If there is anyone to worship and adore, it is you.

If there is anyone to honor and listen to, it is you.

If there is anyone you wish to give your love and devotion to, give it to you.

If there is anyone's wisdom you are desiring to hear, may it be your own.

Many of us have empowered everything outside of ourselves, and so little within ourselves.

It's time for that to change. It's time for you to realize that you are the greatest teacher, the greatest guru. You have within you the greatest of wisdoms; you are all that you have been looking for, all you have been wanting to experience. Everything you have been seeking, it is all there within you.

This recognition is part of the shift we are experiencing on our planet. We are coming to the end of spirituality as we have known it, the end of spirituality as a hierarchy of teachers and students, gurus and seekers. With enlightenment, people discover the full connection to who and what they are, and become empowered in their identity. We will no longer need spiritual teachers to remind us who we are; we will no longer need guidance or reassurance from external sources.

When you experience yourself *as the Divine*, you have access to the same gifts, potentials and abilities that all of the great teachers have possessed. With this experience, this Divine knowing, we understand and remember what spirituality is really about: loving and accepting everything, completely, without conditions.

This is how the Divine loves! Unconditionally, with complete acceptance.

Reaching the place of unconditional love is a process, a journey of experience and development. There is no way of predicting how long this journey will take - it takes as long as it needs to take, and goes wherever it needs to go. Whatever experience you need to have will be there.

Learning to love, accept and trust the process without longing for the destination is part of the journey; it teaches you to love and accept on a higher level, without conditions. As the True You continues to unfold, your vibration becomes so high, and your life is so in the flow that you will not feel the need to seek any outside authorities for assistance.

Practice this now, even as you read this book. Listen to your own guidance, do what feels right for you. You know your own heart. Do what you are guided and lead to do!

My desire for you? I want you to have such a close and personal relationship with the Divine that you are able to get your questions answered by going within yourself. I want you to be so tuned into the Divine that you are able to maintain higher vibrations on your own, and you no longer need me, or any other teachers or guides. You will simply, easily be out in the world, living, creating, exploring and enjoying your life as the Divine in human form.

I want you to always remember to look within for guidance, for blessings, for understanding.

Look within first. Look within always.

Setting Mile-Markers for Reflection

As you work your way through this book, you'll make steady but subtle progress - sometimes so subtle that you may not even notice the changes.

Being human, we often need proof of our progress, a way to measure results of our efforts. Take the time now to set a few intentions and goals, and you'll have milestones to help you measure your progress as you reflect back on how far you've truly come!

You've probably already made several lists of intentions and goals for your life; you know the drill, and you may be tired of the practice. But what I'm asking you to do is different! This list is not of things you're going to actively strive for, but more like wishes for things you'd like to have just happen in your life, things you'd like to be surrounded by in your world. It's like setting mile-markers along a path, markers that, when you reach them, will be the "evidence" that your mind yearns for.

Remember that enlightenment is a process, a never-ending unfolding of who you are. Enlightenment is not a destination, and the path to it cannot be measured because you will never "be there". There is no point in racing from one goal to the next, trying to reach a non-existent finish line. Enlightenment is never completed, so enjoy the journey, revel in each element of growth. Setting your mile-markers will help you recognize those moments of growth that deserve celebration.

So if you'll get out a piece of paper and a pen, we'll walk through this exercise together. Ready? Let's begin with today's date, on the top of the page.

Now, pause for a moment and think about what you want for your life. Think about how you want to feel. Let your mind wander, imagine, let yourself dream. Don't worry about what you think is possible or probable. Think BIG!

As soon as the ideas start to flow, write them down, without censoring or judging them. Record the images that pass through your mind's eye, record the details of how you want to feel.

Got those ideas flowing from your mind to the paper? Great!

If you're a little stuck, that's ok too.

Here are a few nudges to help you refine your mile-stones; try to answer as many of these as you can. If any feel too uncomfortable, it's alright to leave them blank for now. You can always come back and add more later on down the road.

- What things do you want in your life? What do you want to attract and manifest in the world around you? (It's fine to want physical items; the Divine does not judge our desires, but simply wants them to be met)

- What feelings do you want to experience? What emotions do you want to flow through your world?

- What are the challenges, struggles and issues in your life that you'd like to see resolved, overcome, dissolved? What would that feel like?

- Is there anything in your world, an emotion, a memory, a relationship, a need that you'd like to release, to let go of permanently?

- Can you see what you want your life to look like, six months from now, a year from now, five years? Where do you live, what are you doing?

- What do you want your relationships to look like? Would you like changes in your primary relationships, or to develop new ones?

- How do you envision your health, what changes and improvements would you like to see? What does being healthy look like and feel like to you?

- What do you want from your career? How do you want to feel about it, what does it look like, what sorts of contributions does your ideal vocation make to your life, to your world?

- What do you want to see in your spiritual life? What sorts of experiences, growth and changes do you want from your spiritual side?

- How would you like to spend your leisure time? What would a full and satisfying social life look like to you?

- Is there anything else you'd like to see changed in your world, anything else you'd like to have or experience in your life?

There... that wasn't so hard, was it? Now put this away somewhere safe, maybe sealed in an envelope. Date the outside of it, for a day three months from now.

When those three months have passed, open the envelope, and re-read these goals and intentions. Revel in how much has shifted for you, how much progress you've made towards them, without spending your conscious attention making it happen!

This reflection, these mile-markers will provide the evidence of change for you; it's necessary, because the mind isn't always able to grasp the changes on the level that they're happening. The mind will likely try to dismiss the truth and beauty of your progress, to dismiss the changes as random, flukes, or coincidences. Armed with these measurable milestones, you'll be able to *prove* to yourself that this process is *real*, that it *works*, that it is *different*, and best of all, that it works without you struggling and striving for the results.

The change just happens!

Congratulations on setting your milestones!

Wasn't that easy?

Life Should Always Be Easy!

When I give Grace Blessings, I let go and allow the Divine Presence to work through me. I surrender completely to it, and get myself out of the way. I am present, of course, and aware, but no action on my part is required. I simply sit back and enjoy the sensations that pass through my body as the energy flows.

I don't have to do anything at all, it is so easy! I do not need to know the details of a situation or problem; no one has to reveal embarrassing or scary details, and no one needs to revisit painful places in their memories in order for them to be resolved. I don't need to understand the mechanism through which this happens, and neither does the recipient. It just happens. It's that easy.

During the silent retreats I hold, I initiate others into Grace Blessings, so that the energy can be transmitted through them, as well. The Initiation ceremony is quite magical, and a great deal of it is like the Blessings themselves - it just happens! It magically, easily, flows through me, but it is not about me, not at all. Parts of the ceremony do require my more active participation, but those parts are for the benefit of our more human, conscious minds, so that we will accept what is happening.

Once this ceremonial part is done, each participant steps forward to the altar and they receive their Initiation from the Divine directly. This is not an initiation I give; no human being can give it. The Initiation into Grace Blessings is gifted personally from Source. It is powerful, it is real, and it is easy. All that is required is that we open to receive it and get out of the way. How simple!

The ceremony works, even though I have no solid understanding of how it works. And I don't need to understand! Not understanding is perfectly ok, and I accept that. I let go and allow it to be done for me. It's easy.

Let this process be easy for you, too.

Let life be easy for you.

You may have beliefs that life is hard and life is a struggle. You may even have a lot of evidence that you believe *proves* it is a struggle; many of us spend our lives collecting evidence for our beliefs. And that's ok. A belief is simply a thought that we've held in our minds for a long while, something we've convinced ourselves is true. But beliefs can change! Open your thoughts to the possibility of a different belief, the possibility that life can be easy and joyful.

Just be open to the possibility, that is all I ask of you. If you cannot be open, that is ok too. Just be wherever you are with your beliefs, for now. Keep reading, and let Grace show you how different life can be despite your skepticism. Because while you've been collecting your evidence that life is a struggle, I've been collecting evidence that life is easy!

The energy speaks for itself, so I will carry you with my full faith and belief until you can walk on your own two feet in the knowing that life can be different. Life does not need to be a struggle.

Life can be, should be, fun, effortless, and *easy*!

Shifting Your Consciousness

Take note of this quote from Albert Einstein; we'll come back to it many times:

> *"A problem cannot be solved from the*
> *same consciousness in which it was created."*

Shifting our energy changes our consciousness; when we shift our consciousness, our problems shift too, without effort. When we want to solve a problem, we must change our energy *first,* and then the solutions follow naturally.

Taking a lot of frantic action does not often help solve problems. If our vibration is not aligned with our desire, adding more action just expends energy with little return. But when we line up our energy first, the manifestation will follow. Remember: Shift the energy, shift the issue. It really is that simple.

The Grace Blessings that you are receiving as you read will help you to shift your inner world and expand your consciousness. You do not have to work at this; your job is to let go and allow the Divine to do the work for you.

The Formula for Success Is *"Let Go and Let God"*

When you get in the flow of life, abundance showers upon you. What you need comes to you, when you need it, allowing you to relax, knowing that all is well, always.

The day I was writing this chapter, I needed a little extra money for some purchases I wanted to make. Unexpectedly, I received a phone call from a man who had taken a seminar with me. He owed me money for products and services that I'd given him, and he wanted to pay me, right then! The money came in just when I needed it. This is what happens when we are in the flow, this is what happens when we are able to get out of the way, and *"Let go and let God."*

So in this book, I am not going to ask you to work on anything in your life; I am only going to ask you to "Let go and let God". The Blessings you receive as you read will help the True You to blossom naturally, without effort, without trying. As you remember who you really are, your thoughts, words and actions will begin to match that Truth. Life becomes easy, effortless and beautiful.

Please allow yourself to receive all of the support you need as you progress. Allow yourself to ask for and accept help until you are able to maintain the higher vibrations on your own, consistently. The more readily and easily you can "let go", the better, but there is no need to rush things! Everyone's timetable with this is different.

Using Your Free Will

There is very little you need to actually *do* as this process of Enlightenment unfolds. One thing you can do is use your free will to choose to let go consciously, and wisely. You can also use your free will to be sure that you choose empowering thoughts, rather than disempowering ones.

At first, your mind (also known as your False Self or ego) may struggle against letting go and surrendering. But once you start, you will quickly find that you don't have as many negative thoughts and feelings as before. The little monsters in your head disappear. The constant nagging worries cease, and you'll breathe a sigh of relief at the freedom you'll find without them. So use your conscious choices to stay in the flow of Grace, actively choose to let go, even though your mind may try to fight it.

Grace will do most of this for you. The process laid out in this book is the easiest path I know. You only need to choose to walk down it, to choose to let it be easy, to choose thoughts that empower the True You.

It is your choice.

Moving into Acceptance, Letting Go of Resistance

A major step toward revealing the True You is developing a practice of acceptance. Throughout our lives, we learn to resist things that are uncomfortable, things we think are not right, things that are not socially acceptable. Our feelings and emotions are among the things we resist most often, and accepting them can be particularly difficult.

In order to progress, we must feel our feelings - all of them, without exception.

Try this, as an experiment:
As feelings and emotions come up, don't fight them. Allow them to rise, allow yourself to experience them without resistance or judgment. Judgment is like quicksand, it pulls you down, until you are stuck in the feeling and emotion. The more you judge an emotion as bad or negative, the more you resist it, the more deeply mired in it you become.

This can feel suffocating, like you are trapped by the emotions and the suffering they cause. But the emotions themselves don't bring the suffering; it is the resistance to emotions that brings suffering!

Allow the feelings to exist, allow them to be what they are, and they will flow on through you. Remove the judgment, and the quicksand will dissolve. Stop resisting, stop fighting the emotions, and the uncomfortable feelings will flow easily. Let go of your resistance, and the quicksand will become like clear water, allowing you and your emotions to move freely.

Like the rest of this journey, acceptance is a process; there are always new revelations that we'll find ourselves resistant to, new realities about ourselves and the world that we are hesitant to accept.

Consider this scenario:
You wake up one morning, and look outside the window to see what the day is like. It's gray and cloudy. "Blech," you think to yourself. "Why can't it be sunny?" You start the day a bit grumpy, because things aren't the way you want them. As the day goes on, you continue to resist the way things are, and maybe it even starts to rain! You judge the clouds as "bad weather", and grumble some more.

But your judgment and resistance and grumbling don't change the weather, they don't magically dissolve the clouds. In fact, the only effect your judgments really seem to have is on your mood, and by now, you're feeling *really* grumpy.

But what if something changed? What if you noticed that you were in a place of resistance? What if you decided to let go, accepted the day without judgment? What do you think would happen to your mood, then?

You could even take this a step further, as I have - what if you accepted that weather, and even life, are impermanent? What if you told yourself "I may have preferred sunshine today, but I accept the weather as it is, now. Weather always changes, as life always changes, and it will be sunny again sometime soon." What do you think would happen to your grumpiness if you tried this approach?

You might discover, as I did, that *your natural state is happiness.* You might realize that any feeling other than peaceful contentment is only temporary. You might begin to find that the True You *is* happy, and content!

The True You springs from a place of acceptance. All you need to do is to stop resisting. Trust in the natural flow, and it will happen.

When Not to Simply Accept

Of course, if there is something you can do about outside circumstances, by all means, be the agent of positive change!   Part of acceptance is the recognition that life and circumstances are always changing; there's no reason you cannot be an active part of that change. So when things are outside of your control (like the weather) practice accepting them. When things are within your control (like your mood) take supportive action on what you can, and accept the results. Acceptance makes things easy, resistance makes things difficult, and causes suffering.

Another Exercise:
In Chandra Alexander's book, *Reality Works*, she shares a method she uses to work with emotions. It is simple and effective; I encourage you to use it. When an unwanted feeling or emotion arises, sit down in that moment and allow yourself to experience and feel it fully. You may find that some deep, meditative breathing will help you to sit with it more easily.

As the feeling becomes stronger, speak to it, strike up a conversation with it. Tell the feeling, "Hey there, fear, anger, irritation (or whatever emotion it is)... here I am, right here. I won't run from you, and I am listening. I apologize if I haven't been listening to you much, but I am here now. You have my full attention. Please get as strong as you possibly can. I want to feel you *intensely.*"

Then let the feelings intensify, as wildly as they will! Allow the sensations to have their way with you (so to speak!). As you remove your resistance this way, inviting the emotion to manifest fully, you'll notice something interesting: any emotion that you allow yourself to feel fully, without restriction, will move up in vibration. As it moves up in vibration, it will shift and dissipate on its own, without any effort from you. It will simply go away. Like so many other things in this book, there is no timetable for how long the change will take. Let the emotions shift and move in their own time, as you welcome them.

When you notice the emotion beginning to change and dissolve, tell it that you will welcome it back, any time. This way you are not resisting your emotions; you are not pushing against them, but staying open and practicing acceptance.

Don't be alarmed if during the exercise, your emotions shift from one to another. You may start off with an anxious feeling, then it may become fear, then anger, and so on. Allow all the feelings to move and change as they will. *This is the key to your freedom.*

Later in this book we will give you a more detailed process to help you deal with your emotions even more thoroughly, but this is a great exercise whenever unwanted emotions arise. It's also a great process to try when you're feeling positive emotions, too! Give yourself over to happiness and joy, allowing them to intensify and expand, and see what happens then!

Let Go and Let God

You've probably heard the phrase *"Let Go, and Let God"* many times in your life, but maybe never paid it much attention or really understood it. It's just another way of describing the process in this book.

"Let go" means releasing resistance, letting go of the past pains, burdens, resentments and baggage. It means accepting things as they are, whether they are within or out of your control.

"Let God" means allowing the Divine to do the work, allowing yourself to accept the Blessings.

Some people ask, "Why do we need to actively 'let go, and let God?' Why do we need to practice acceptance? Why can't the Divine just do all of it for us?"

We have been given the gift of freewill, and the Divine will not take that away from us. Whether we make good decisions or poor ones, whether we make choices that raise our vibrations or lower them, they are our decisions, our choices, our will. This is a very important, empowering gift.

We can use our free will to decide how much control we're willing to let go of at any given time; we can use our free will to allow the Divine to lead us, guide us and direct us, or to choose the degree of control we will turn over.

Your False Self may not like this idea much; it fears the unknown, it fears being out of control. So take the time to soothe that part of yourself; give yourself the care and nurturing you have always craved.

Maybe you've wished you could have more love and care from your parents, lovers, partners and friends. Maybe you just wanted more love and acceptance from the world around you, as a whole. We often look outside of ourselves to have our needs met. We look to others to make ourselves feel complete. But this doesn't work, it only gives our power away, making us feel even more incomplete. The more incomplete we feel, the more the False Self will scramble for control.

So learn this: Whatever your needs are, they can be met from within yourself. Practice giving all of the love, gentleness, warmth and support that you freely give to others to yourself; give it in whatever ways feel appropriate and right. Let go of that desire to have your needs met from outside, and allow the needs to be met from within. All parts of yourself (even the false ones) will be more comfortable and easier to live with this way. Meet your needs from within yourself, and you'll find that "letting go and letting God" becomes easier. Meet your needs from within yourself, and surrendering to the flow of life and blessings begins to feel natural, instead of scary.

But if you are still in a place of fear, don't worry. Just be extremely easy and gentle on yourself. Wherever you are, that is ok. Remember to practice acceptance, and release resistance. The practice of "letting go and letting God" is about letting go of our resistance, and opening up to really *living*. Whatever your challenges or struggles are, approach them with acceptance, and give them over to the Divine. Let Grace carry you. Your external circumstances will shift; they always do. Approaching your life with an attitude of letting go will help circumstances to shift more easily, with less effort - if circumstances even require any effort from you at all!

Once you begin to experience the elegance and simplicity of this process, you'll find yourself trusting in it more and more. I assure you, this will make it easier for you to let go. It is a process, like everything else in this book.

Prayer as a Tool for "Letting Go and Letting God"

During meditation, I used to hear the following words in my mind over and over, "Speak the word and you shall be healed." This was a message to me about prayer, and using the creative and spiritual power of the spoken word.

When we're troubled, we want to take action, to *do* something to make ourselves feel better. Prayer is an action. It is something we can do, a change we can make to immediately bring some relief. Some people approach prayer as if it were passive, but it is *action.*

Remember how Einstein said that no problem can be solved in the same consciousness in which it was created? Prayer changes your consciousness; it causes shifts in your thinking. When your thinking shifts, the reality of the problems and troubles shifts, too, and the solutions begin to fall into place.

But prayer does more than just shift your consciousness. When you pray, you connect with Source energy. When you pray, the force of that energy works within you, through you, moving powerfully into the world around you.

Prayer is a triple action; it is asking, communing and receiving all at once. Prayer happens in the mind, and the mind is the connecting agent that links God and humans; it creates a free-flowing channel of energy between us and the Divine. Opening that channel makes our lives so much easier!

I have personally experienced time and again; when I stop, pray and meditate before taking further action, I get more accomplished with less energy and with greater ease and flow.

When you allow prayer to be the first action you take, when you make the effort to sit, be still, and go within through prayer, you open to Divinely inspired ideas and solutions. You won't hear the voice of the Infinite when you are running around like a chicken with your head cut off! Take the time to calm yourself, ask, commune, and listen through prayer. Prayers release God-power, and the sooner you begin praying on a problem, the sooner the Divine will manifest, lining up the people, events and circumstances for the highest benefit of all involved.

People often say that we only use about 10% of our brain power and potential. Where is the other 90%? It is that huge, often untapped part of us that is Source energy. When we get still, go within, and pray, we commune with Source within us. We do not just *have* unlimited potential, we *are* unlimited potential. When we line up our energy with that potential, when we use prayer to go within, we don't waste our energy through outward, unguided expression. When we let go of our desire to take problem-solving action on our own, and take the time to let God work through us and through our prayers, everything comes so much easier.

Release the resistance, accept the need to take action by praying. Speak the word, and you shall be healed. Let go, and let God.

Claim the "I AM"

The most powerful prayers I have ever found begin with "I AM" statements. Because the Divine is within us, when we speak the words, "I AM", it is the same thing as saying, "God in me IS _____." Using the phrase "I AM" to begin an affirmative prayer speaks to the energy and essence of God's spark within you. It becomes a Divine command, and reality obeys that command.

"I AM" statements are among the most powerful prayers you can make. They affirm and direct the power of God within you. Even when you feel negative, or when you struggle with limiting beliefs, prayers of "I AM" will work to redirect you in a positive, affirmative way.

Below are some examples to try; speak them slowly, one at a time. Let yourself *feel* their power and strength.

- "I AM Beauty"

- "I AM Compassion"

- "I AM Whole"

- "I AM Prosperity"

- "I AM the Light of the World"

- "I AM open and say Yes to life"

- "I AM the fulfillment of all of my wants, needs and desires of this day"

- "I AM perfect sight and hearing"

- "I AM the manifest perfection of health"

- "I AM abundant supply"

- "I AM peace of mind, body and spirit"

- "I AM clarity and focus"

- "I AM infinite love, joy and happiness"

- "I AM surrendering the totality of my being to the God Presence within me now"

- "I AM surrendering this issue to the light within me now, manifesting perfect outcomes for all involved"

Create some of your own "I AM" statements. Use them to direct the Source energy within you. These powerful statements work unlike anything I have ever experienced; they can help shift your thoughts and mood instantaneously. "I AM" statements help you to become what you want to be.

"I AM" Statements Create a Space of Being

This is difficult to put into words, but it is something that you can feel the truth in, if you let yourself contemplate it. Speaking the phrase "I AM Beauty" creates the space for you to not only have beauty, but to *be* Beauty. By saying the words "I AM Healed", you do not just experience healing, you become the healing. You are *being* healed, *being* the healer, being the *healing* itself.

A state of "being" exists before anything manifests in the physical world. Before anything can happen in the world, it first has to enter a state of "being". The energy of "being" creates the space for the having, or doing. You can remember this as "Energy first, manifestation follows."

"Being" speaks to the heart of what you desire, without getting mired in the details of how it will happen, or what it will look like. Everything flows from that state of being; it sets the energy for the manifestation. If fulfilling your desires were a puzzle, the state of being creates the table on which the puzzle pieces come together - and once the table is there, God fills in those puzzle pieces for you with ease, elegance, and best of all, *Grace.*

Prayers of "I AM" create the state of being that prepares the way for manifestation. They are a powerful, meaningful way to commune with the Presence of The Divine within you, they are the meaning behind "Speaking the word," and a truly powerful way to "let go and let God."

Letting go may not be easy for you at first, and that is all right. You have so much help and support! You have an edge that most people do not have; you know that Grace is willing to do for you what you cannot humanly do for yourself. Your only job is to let go and let it in.

Letting Go: Learning the Art of Prostration

Prostrate: To lower oneself face down, flat upon the ground, in a display of reverence, humility, submission or adoration.

Prostration is one of the most effective tools we have; it helps us to give over to the Divine Presence whatever is too large for us. It is a simple, physical act that tells the body to relax, and tells the mind to let go. Prostration gets us out of the way so that miracles can happen. Your mind may resist that idea right now, but once you've experienced the process and the *results* of prostration, you'll better understand its power, and why I place so much importance on it.

The form of prostration I suggest is both physical and mental/spiritual. First, you physically lower yourself to the ground, and then, you mentally and spiritually lay any and all burdens at the feet of the Divine. Those burdens can include your struggles, conflicts, turmoil, resistance, confusion and anything that feels too heavy or too big for you.

* * *

Step by Step, the Process of Prostrating:

- Get on your knees, close your eyes and begin to take stock of any feeling, knowledge, tension, burden or conflict within your body, mind and spirit that you feel you cannot handle.

- Lean forward, stretching out face down, forehead touching the floor, arms extended overhead in a formal prayer position.

- Relax your body, let the tension drain away. This usually happens naturally in this position; as you let go emotionally, your physical body lets go and you feel more relaxed.
- While you are lying there, speak to the Divine about what is going on. Give everything over, lay it at the feet of the Source.

- Stay in the prostrated position for as long as feels right and necessary for you. You will know when you are done, you will *feel* it.

- When you are ready, get up, dust yourself off and consciously choose to leave your burdens behind. Say to the Divine, "I am letting this all go and giving it all over to you to handle."

- Enjoy! Let your mind dwell on pleasant thoughts, let your body indulge in the sense of lightness, joy and freedom, take part in a physical activity that brings you joy.

It is okay to adapt this practice to make it more accessible to you. For instance, I enjoy envisioning a Divine figure in front of me. I imagine that I am giving everything to them personally to deal with. This makes it more intimate and real for me, and the more real, the more effective. You may also adapt it so it is more comfortable, or to allow for physical limitations: you might want to place a small pillow under your forehead for comfort, or put a prayer mat, folded blanket or pillow under your knees.

The experience of prostrating is unique to each individual, and each instance of prostration. It can be very subtle, or quite intense. Again, let go of expectations, your experience will be perfect for you and different every time you do it.

When you are first training the mind to let go of your burdens and resistance this way, it is very human and natural for the mind to want to try to take back all that you just gave over. That is why I suggest you end by dwelling on pleasant thoughts. But if you do find that you have taken your burdens back, and perhaps are trying to find solutions on your own again, repeat the exercise; prostrate yourself and give it over again, repeatedly.

By choosing to release the burden or problem through prostration repeatedly, you'll raise your vibration above the quicksand, so that your limiting thoughts and worry will shift; you will pull free of the issues this way. Be soft and gentle with yourself, there's no need to struggle - struggle is resistance. Remember that this is a new way of *being,* and though it can take a little time to master, it is well worth the energy and time. Be patient with yourself and the process.

* * *

Release Your Expectations of Results

Prostrating gets your desires and attachments out of the way of the Source Energy, allowing the Divine to manifest some amazing results in your life. You may be tempted to try and rush the process, but all things happen in Divine time. So release your expectations of how long it should take; it will take exactly as long as it needs to, for the most perfect, beneficial result. Wishing or trying to make it happen on *your* timetable adds to resistance and slows the receiving process.

Of course, if you have something urgent demanding attention in your life, it is ok to take action and solve problems on your own. I am not suggesting that you sit on the couch and wait for solutions to fall out of the sky! It is ok to act to create results, just do not rush the Divine manifestation of results, or expect that problems be solved for you on your timetable.

Prostrate yourself, give over the problems, then act upon the *guidance* you receive. Follow the solutions and guidance that feels best to you.

* * *

Sometimes, the Guidance is *"Wait and See."*

In the printing of my first book, *Infinite Blessings,* I encountered a challenge that illustrates how this works. When I submitted the project to the printer, I received a quote for the cost of the first run. The amount felt good to me, so I went ahead with the project.

A few weeks later, I received an e-mail about a potentially serious issue. The quote was wrong! There was a misunderstanding about how many pages the book was, and the agent felt that the cost would be double the amount we'd agreed on. Well this could have changed things quite a bit.

I sat with the problem, got silent, and went within. I immediately heard a number of potential solutions. Most of them felt pretty good but nothing that felt like that "Aha" feeling I was looking for, the one that clearly tells me, "now that is the way to go."

I decided to prostrate, and give it over to the Divine. I did not speak much about the potential problem with my friends or peers, because I knew those conversations would give the problem more reality than was necessary. I didn't want my focus to be on the problem, but on opening myself to the solution!

I spoke with the editor friend who had been working with me, and we decided to let it go, give it to the Divine to solve. We released it over the weekend.

Monday afternoon came, and I received another e-mail from the printer. They were able to shift things around, and keep the cost about the same, with only an insignificant increase! The printer pointed out to me, "Erica, this book is not even printed yet and you are already manifesting a Divine Intervention!" Yes, I surely did, and how amazing that even he recognized that!

I let go, prostrated, gave it over to the Divine and had a "wait and see attitude."

Wait and see are three powerful words; use them!

* * *

More Personal Experience

The first time I prostrated, when my head rested on the floor, I wept tears of relief. Before that moment I was unaware that I had fallen into the trap of trying to do it all, figure it all out and know it all. As I stayed in that position, this immense burden slowly lifted off of my body. I was so relieved to feel, *to know,* that here was this all powerful, loving, all knowing being that loved me, wanted for me, cherished me and was delighted and capable of handling all of the details of my life.

I knew right then, there was no problem too big nor too small; that the Divine would take care of it for me. I just had to let go, to create an opening for miracles to occur.

My physical body reacted strongly; first, it tensed up. Then, as I began my deep breathing, my body shook, then slowly began to relax, bit by bit, letting go. Gradually, my mind also let go, until it went blank. It went so blank that when I finally got up off of the floor I could not even remember what had been burdening me! It was gone, wiped from my memory.

This was exciting, so freeing! Now I knew why this ancient act of prostration is used by traditions all over the world, in many forms. Some traditions prostrate to their gurus, or to an altar. Others visualize a Divine figure before them, as I do. Adapt it as it suits you - you can even prostrate and ask for advice on how to best prostrate!

* * *

When You Should Prostrate

Please try this *Now!*

Take everything that is burdening you and lay it all down at the feet of the Divine.

I cannot say enough about how important this one act is. It works! If you are at a crossroads in your life and you don't know what to do, PROSTRATE. Feel overwhelmed, PROSTRATE. Feel lousy all around, PROSTRATE. Lose your job, PROSTRATE. Diagnosed with a disease, PROSTRATE. Having relationship difficulties, PROSTRATE. Have an influx of painful childhood memories, PROSTRATE!

Do you get the idea? Do this whenever and wherever you find yourself burdened or confused. When you find yourself feeling overwhelmed or overly concerned with the details of your life, lay down, and lay it down. Prostrate, let go.

Learning to let go is an art form and this is the simplest and most effective way I know to develop that art form. Prostration tells the body to let go, it instructs the mind to let go. Once you lay all of your struggles and burdens at the feet of the Divine you will be amazed at how much peace you have, how much energy you have. When you are not weighted down with all of that heaviness your walking in lighter loafers, walking on air! The heaviness lifts, and your experience becomes Heavenly!

* * *

An Example from My Life

Recently, I was looking for a new place to live. I found an ad for a great place, but they said no pets. My cat companion, Spirit, is non- negotiable in my life; he is with me until he chooses otherwise. Talking to the landlord, I found that her resistance to pets was that she'd just spent a significant amount of money on new carpet for the entire place. She'd had a tenant's cat damage things before, and she was worried she'd lose her investment in the new carpet.

I knew that trying harder to convince her or manipulating her was not the answer; I wanted a solution that would be a win for everyone, an answer that would give the landlady the peace of mind she needed. I decided to just let it go, give the situation over to the Presence and wait to see what would happen. I made a simple quick prayer about it, and released it.

The next day I was doing my cardio-session at the gym, and began daydreaming about a home I had many years ago. I remembered having renter's insurance when I lived there, and suddenly, it clicked! If I had renter's insurance, it would give the landlord the extra reassurance she was looking for. If there was damage to her carpet, the insurance would replace it!   I called her right away and shared my solution. She was fine with it, and fully open to accepting me and Spirit into her rental home. It was that easy!

Notice that I didn't go looking for a solution, and I didn't know where the solution would come from. I simply turned the problem over to the

Divine, got out of the way, went on with my life. The solution just appeared.

This is the way life goes when you are in the flow and allow Grace to carry you; solutions just fall into your lap.

If we can slow down enough, get quiet and go within, all of the answers we seek are there. Solutions may not bubble up to the surface instantaneously, though they can. Sometimes the solutions we seek come from another person, event or circumstance seemingly out of nowhere. You will see this more and more often. This translates to everything in our inner and outer world when we allow Grace in.

* * *

Another Example

Below is an e-mail I received from a client who bought my "Infinite Blessings" music CD. The music, like this book, has been infused with Divine Grace, and initiates the Enlightenment process. After using it for just a week, here is what she had to say:

"I've listened to your CD every night right before I turn off the light to sleep for about a week. I listen to one or two tracks each night. I choose the ones I feel will encourage sleep, which has always been difficult for me. I've waited this long to write to you because I wanted to see if my experiences were a fluke or if maybe your music and blessings had some influence on my life.

I've found that life has suddenly become easier somehow. Since I started listening to your CD, solutions to work problems have appeared, I suddenly found something valuable I'd lost (and searched high and low for) and my anxiety level around certain situations has decreased. I've had some really good ideas about work (I'm a special ed case manager in a high school and my case load of 20 students is varied, challenging and delightful) that just suddenly appeared. I wish I could explain myself more eloquently, but really, this is what's been happening: situations that were bumpy have become smoother.

I chose your CD because it seemed like a good complement to another addition in my life. I've started meditating again after letting my practice lapse for a long, long time. I think I'm on the right track overall.

Thank you so much for sharing whatever it is you do! I have no idea what you mean when you say blessings can be communicated through your music, but something is definitely happening. Again, thank you so very much."

This is a perfect example of solutions just showing up without working on them. You really do not have to work harder, fix it all, know it all and figure it all out. The Divine will do it for you; your job is to let the Blessings in!

Are You Ready for Your First Grace Blessing?

With Grace, we have access to unlimited possibilities and infinite love. The direct, Divine experience of Grace Blessings can set us free from old patterns, programming and limiting beliefs. It has the power to to reestablish our health, to manifest our highest dreams. Grace Blessings contain the potential to make anything happen, outside of the limits of time. We don't need to worry about it, or direct it - The Divine energy itself decides what will be given to us, and when. The results often exceed what our limited minds have has asked for! By experiencing the Source in this way, we open up unimagined potential for ourselves and the world!

Our minds cannot comprehend this pure potential. The human brain is designed to question, label, categorize, break down and organize information in a linear way. Our culture trains our mind to believe that we must make plans and take action to attain our dreams. But the Source doesn't operate in such a step by step, limited manner! It operates outside of time, outside of space.

Through my experience with Grace Blessings, I have become a conduit for that Divine, unlimited energy. It lifts me to a state of potential where instantaneous change can occur, beyond our limited ideas of possibility. During Grace Blessing transmissions I am anchored in this limitless energy. There is no uncertainty in me about it - I have an absolute knowledge that this experience is real, and true.

The Divine already knows your heart's true desire; setting an intention or goal is not necessary. But if you'd like to make a specific request or set a focus before receiving a Grace Blessing, that's perfectly ok. Some people even bring photos of family, children and pets to sessions, with the hope that their loved ones will be positively affected by the Blessing, too; they've reported positive, even miraculous seeming results.

To focus the Blessing, quietly make your request in a way that is comfortable to you, then let it go. Release it. Let the energy flow through you, without directing it. Hold your mind open like a child's, free from your adult mind's desire to know and control how the solution will play out. The Divine carries the responsibility for determining what you receive and when; you need only to open yourself to all possibilities.

In the first chapter of this book, I asked you to say Yes! to the changes that would be coming your way through this material. Now, I'm asking you to say *Yes! a*gain, this time specifically to the experience of this Grace Blessing.

Let Go, Let it In Now!

The image below is infused with Divine Energy; the Blessings it carries will begin the process of your Enlightenment. The artist, Sven Geier, entitled this particular piece "Heaven". Appropriate, isn't it? Grace Blessings open the crown chakra, allowing Grace to flow down through you, as if from Heaven.

To receive the Blessing in this and the other art in the book, just let your relaxed gaze fall on it easily and gently. I suggest gazing at each piece of art for a period of about two minutes. Contemplate and reflect on the image and whatever feelings come up for you for a few moments. When you feel the experience is complete, please close your eyes and rest, lying down for at least fifteen to twenty minutes, and longer if time allows.

Receive the blessing, and then experience, and feel.

Congratulations!
You have just received your first Grace Blessing!

This is more exciting than you may know. After I opened to Grace, my life changed and has never been the same since! I delight in helping others and live to serve. I imagine a world where everyone is fully awake, imagine how we can create Heaven right here on Earth. Thank you for joining me.

From now on you can have an experience of the Divine any time you choose. Connecting with this grand and infinite part of you that is all knowing and all powerful will feel like reuniting with a dear, long lost friend and confidant, and at the same time, it changes everything.

As you read through this book, don't rush your progress. Go at your own pace, and don't get the energy flowing faster in your life than you can assimilate or work through it. I suggest waiting a week between Grace Blessings, but this is only a recommendation. You will know when you are ready for your next blessing. Of course you can go ahead and do the reading in this book, but if you don't feel it is the right time for your next blessing, then skip over the pieces of art contained in the book.

* * *

How The Blessings Are Shared

Grace Blessings can be shared in many different ways. The energy can be infused in physical objects or imagery, as in this book. Grace can be transmitted through music, as with my CDs. In live sessions and workshops, I typically transmit the energy by placing my hands gently on the top of the recipient's head for a few moments. Grace can be given through the eyes, a very powerful, personal form that I use during initiation ceremonies in Silent Retreats. Blessings can also be given just by sitting in the room with a group of people and setting the intention! Proximity is not important; Grace Blessings can be done by phone, even when the recipient is on the other side of the world.

But my favorite way to give Grace Blessings is through hugs - I call them Divine Mother Hugs! These "blessing hugs" are an ancient, cross cultural practice; people from all over the world have received initiations and blessings from their gurus through hugs. Amma, the Hugging Saint, is a modern day example from India; look her up, she does give quite a hug! Grace Blessings are simple to give and receive, and easily accessible no matter where you are.

That doesn't mean the mind has an easy time with them! The effects of a Grace Blessing can be somewhat overwhelming; the mind has no frame of reference for this experience and it is not easy for the mind to maintain an open state of acceptance. As the process of the Blessing and discovering the True You unfolds, you may find some extra support helpful. If you feel the need, I do offer personal coaching sessions either in person, or on the phone. Many people receive all of the support they need just from the material in this book, but do not hesitate to ask for help if you think it might be useful! Do what feels right to you.

Remember that Enlightenment is accessed through the heart, not the mind. Opening your heart to give and receive love freely is hugely liberating. You don't have to try and work on this or do anything to force your heart open; it will fully open and flower in its own time. You cannot force this to happen. No matter how many books you read or workshops you attend, nothing your mind can do will hurry Enlightenment. But if you set your mind aside, be open to letting go of all of your old outdated beliefs and limited concepts about spirituality and the Divine, if you allow yourself to authentically receive without judgment, and let go of the desire to explain or understand what is happening? You become a blank slate for Truth to write upon!

This unfolding of Enlightenment is unlike anything you have ever done or experienced before. Let go of everything you think you know and be open. Look upon everything as if for the first time with baby fresh eyes of wonder. You cannot rush this unfolding, this Enlightenment, but Grace can give it to you instantaneously; you have only to move your mind out of the way and receive the Blessing.

Incorporate this into your day to day life. Practice accepting and receiving, all day every day.

Awareness of the False Self

This book is called The True You, but most of us stumble through life without ever knowing our True Self, living only in a limited shadow of who we really are.

Everyone has different terms for this limited aspect; ego is the most common word used. But however it's described, this false aspect of ourselves is the part that feels disconnected from the Divine. It's this part of ourselves that believes there is such a thing as "not enough", and it's this part of us that believes life is a competition. The False Self is the part that gets defensive, as if something is always "out to get us", or take something away from us.

Do not treat the False Self as bad or wrong. Although it is limited, it is doing the best it can with the tools it has. As you move through Enlightenment, this False Self, the Ego (or whatever you are comfortable calling it) will begin to let go and allow your Divine Self to lead. The False Self may kick up a fight during the letting go process; it may fear that its very existence is in jeopardy. It may believe it needs to fight for its life, it may even believe it is fighting for *your* life.

If that happens, this book will help you through it. Re-read these pages, let them remind you that there is something beyond the False Self, and remember that becoming the True You is an unfolding, not an erasing, of who you have been in the past.

Sometimes, simply being aware of the False Self and its reactions can create a significant shift in your experience. So if you find yourself in sudden resistance and fear, take a few deep breaths, and become aware of what is happening. Once you become aware, you can use your conscious mind and your free will to choose how to respond to the experience. Our greatest power is choice, so choose wisely!

Choose awareness, and soothe the False Self until it can rest in the arms of your Authentic Self, knowing that it will learn to enjoy life from this new place and perspective.

The Grace Blessings you receive in this book will help you become more aware. You do not have to work at this, it happens naturally as the unfolding continues. Awareness is a key part of discovering the True You; without it, we are largely powerless, at the mercy of the forces of our unconscious. But as the process of Grace continues to unfold, you will naturally become increasingly aware of what is true for you and your life. Remember that this truth can seem to shift and change at different levels of consciousness; what is true at one level is not true at another.

As your unfolding continues you will look back over the past days, weeks and months with astonishment at how far you have come, at how much things have shifted and changed for the better without working on anything, just like magic. Even the False Self will come to understand this progress. It, too, will get with the program, and loosen its grip!

This Can Be So Easy!

This journey of unfolding Enlightenment is very simple, if you let it be that way. You decide how difficult it is, you make the choice.

During this process, emotions of every type may emerge; let them! Feelings may seem to arise for no good reason, and sometimes, what we feel may not even be our own emotion, but something we've picked up from the One Mind, the One Mind we're all part of. Just let yourself feel these emotions, it is part of the journey. We are going to discuss emotion and feeling A LOT in this book. You may even feel like I am repeating myself, because I AM! This is for a very good reason, that you will come to understand soon enough.

Know this: *Any feeling that you are willing to fully experience will transform into a better feeling.*

Any emotion that you allow yourself to feel without censorship will raise in vibration, changing it into a more positive experience. If you are willing to take one or two core emotions and dive into them fully, you will eventually master all emotions, completely! It's a great sense of freedom.

Don't worry; you won't have to muddle through every traumatic event, hurt, or disappointment you've been through. One of the radical differences between Grace Blessings and the more familiar methods of therapy is that you don't need to go digging for things to fix, heal and clear. Just receive the Grace Blessings, and allow yourself to fully feel whatever life presents. Let yourself experience whatever feelings come up, and the lower vibrational energies will lift naturally, without you having to do anything.

When you can allow emotions to wash over you freely, without struggling or fighting them, you'll discover a new strength within you:

your feelings will no longer be able to knock you off center. The temptation to judge and criticize your feelings will also fall away, and you'll begin to view emotions as simple experiences to be had, without the extra drama you may be accustomed to.

The key to this elegant, simple process is to drop your resistance to your feelings. If you do not resist, you will be free, no matter what may happen. Do not be afraid to feel! Sometimes, you may find you're afraid of getting stuck in an emotion or negative state; remember that feelings are always fleeting, always changing! The sooner you simply let it be, the sooner it will change, and you will return to being happy again shortly. With a bit of practice, you'll learn to trust this experience. You'll soon recognize that happiness is your natural state, and returning to it is as natural and easy as breathing.

As you learn to simply experience emotions without controlling them, you'll begin to observe yourself as if from a distance, and recognize that the emotions are not really you. This is a truth: You are not your mind, you are not your body, you are not your emotions.

Let that sink in, not as a mental concept, but as a deep inner knowing. Again: *You are not your mind, you are not your body, you are not your emotions.*

Of Lisa and Laughter

Many people report feeling a new intensity in life as their True Self begins to unfold. Mundane life tasks can take on an ecstatic feel, and the lust for life increases. Events that would previously have really bothered you no longer seem so troublesome, and sometimes can even seem humorous.

A student of mine, I will call her Lisa, had received a number of Grace Blessings during a weekly class I was offering. One day, she was making out a grocery list, and spontaneously broke into ecstatic bliss and laughter! She said that it was as if she were watching herself planning lunches, and it just seemed so funny she couldn't stop laughing. She rode the bliss and humor for a long while that afternoon, just sitting on her couch and letting it have its way with her! When the laughter finally passed, she resumed her day and her grocery list writing.

This often happens to me, too; the littlest thing strikes me funny these days and I'll have a good laugh all by myself. In the middle of ordinarily boring life chores, I slip into ecstatic bliss for no good reason, just like Lisa.

It reminds me of being a child. We laughed so much as little children; everything in life was new and funny and silly. Then we grew up and got oh-so-serious! I think that as we move toward our True Selves, back to that open state of acceptance, we begin to see things through a child's eyes again. Life is just funnier seen that way.

So don't be alarmed if this happens to you; it's perfectly normal. Enjoy the ride! Eventually, the intensity of your Enlightenment will smooth out. The ups and downs will even out and be replaced with equanimity - a calm, even temperament. Equanimity comes from a place of acceptance, a place of non-resistance, feeling neutral about whatever happens around you. Once you reach that place, it will be harder and harder to upset you, and if it does happen, the sense of disturbance won't last for long.

The Art of Appreciation

As you start to experience more of the "good" in your life, many doors will start to open for you. Life simply gets easier. You will experience more synchronicities, and you will find yourself flowing through life with tremendous ease and peace.

Take the time to recognize these triumphs! Acknowledge every victory, every success, every drop of good that happens to you. No matter how big or small it seems, sing out to the heavens your recognition of how good life is becoming! I want you to wring out all the juice of the good that is coming to you, so that you can receive every drop. By acknowledging each bit of goodness, you will encourage more, allowing you to ride the wave of goodness for as long as possible.

So rave, rave, *rave* about the experiences you are having! I want you to fully appreciate everything, everything, *everything* that is *good* in your life! Make a huge stinking deal about even the tiniest thing. Celebrate it!

No, you don't need to telephone all of your friends and brag - that would be a bit obnoxious, wouldn't it? Celebrate in private, and take your happiness to the Presence, to the Source. Thank the Source for all that has been happening for you, all that is shifting for the positive!
When you focus this intensely on the positive, through reflecting on it, appreciating it, celebrating it? You bring more and more of it into your world. Life gets sweeter and sweeter, just by thinking on it and being grateful for it. .

An Exercise in Appreciation
(to help you let in more to appreciate!)

I want you to do the following exercise every day, for at least the next 30 days. Say yes to this, now, please!

Each night, before you go to bed, practice prostrating to the Divine; give over everything that has happened in your day. As you finish, turn your attention to all of the wonderful things that you have in your life, all of the current blessings. No matter how hard life may seem, there are always blessings we can appreciate. Some simple examples might include your warm and comfy bed, the softness of your pillow, the health you *do* have, whatever you love most about your animal companions. Think about any qualities you appreciate in your partner, or friends, or co-workers. Consider whatever level of wealth you do have, small things you enjoy about your job - anything and everything that you can appreciate. As you finish, set an intention to sleep restfully and awaken rejuvenated and inspired for the day - allowing you to have even more to appreciate tomorrow!

When you do this practice of appreciation, miracles *will* occur in your life. I am so certain that you will see such radical results, and so soon, that I'm sure you will want to continue long after the 30 days have passed.

The Importance of Feeling

Before I was initiated to give Grace Blessings, I was aware that something was holding me back. I was also aware that I was afraid to really feel my emotions. I feared that if I really let myself "go there" I might just get stuck in that feeling forever, or that it would totally possess and consume me. I did not fully understand at this point that all emotion is fleeting, that it would be impossible to "get stuck" in a feeling forever. I did not understand yet that my natural state is *happiness* and that I would return to that natural state easily if I would just allow myself to authentically *feel*. Happiness eluded me, due to my resistance to fully feeling my feelings! The thing I wanted most was always an arm's length away because of my fear of feeling. Can you relate?

I also knew that I was tired of feeling yanked around by outer circumstances, people and events, of allowing them to influence my mood so strongly. I wanted *ALL* of my power back.

So at a silent retreat, I set an intention to master my mind and emotions once and for all. I wanted to be at peace with how I was feeling, no matter what the circumstances. There were other things I desired, too, of course, there always are. But I gave the control of the results over to the Presence, the Source, knowing that I would receive from this retreat exactly what I needed. I was aware that I had forgotten the Truth of my being, and I knew that through the silence of the retreat, and all of the Grace Blessings I was receiving, I would remember who *"I AM"*. And that is exactly what I received - the knowledge of my True Self.

But I received *so very much more*, and because of that, I can help others to remember their Selves, as well. It was all because I opened myself to fully feel whatever I was presented with in that silent retreat and I continue to practice this every single day of my life.

About Empathic Sensitivity

Throughout my life, I have always been overly sensitive to others' emotions and moods. Going into public places was brutal for me in my earlier and teen years, because I fought and resisted everything I was feeling both from within myself, and from others.

If I would have just allowed myself to feel everything, to accept it and let it flow through and around me, shifting its vibration and mine as it went, nothing would have been able to stick. Life would have been so much easier and more comfortable!

If you are naturally empathic, it is especially important that you allow yourself to fully feel whatever comes to you. Become translucent and allow everything to flow through you, and you will find that you are much freer.

Sometimes, we try to go over, around, or under emotions, instead of having to feel them. Even though I was always spiritually-minded, I did this, too. This is called a "spiritual bypass" and it doesn't work!

A spiritual bypass is any method or trick that keeps you from being real with your emotion. If you've read even one self-help book, you're probably doing a spiritual bypass on your emotions - that is what most books teach. Putting someone who has hurt you in a pink bubble, sending them love and light, picturing their aura filled with little hearts and smiley faces? All of these are spiritual bypasses. They're meant to make you feel better, but in reality, they just get in the way of feeling better!

If you do a spiritual bypass instead of dealing with your emotions, you are not being authentic or real with yourself. In fact, by using these tricks to avoid having to feel, you're at war with your True Self, resisting who you are, denying your real experience. You cannot feel peace when you are at war with yourself. Stop the war, stop bypassing your emotions! You are human, and it is perfectly OK to feel human emotions, even uncomfortable ones.

In order to live in love, bliss and joy, we have to embrace the full human experience and allow all of our emotions to flow. We cannot deny parts of ourselves and expect to become enlightened, happy and free.

Enlightenment involves fully accepting, embracing and loving the totality of being human.

* * *

Get Real with How You Feel, That's the Deal!

Before I understood all of this, I struggled so much with being human; I didn't like the game I'd come here to play. But when I opened to Grace, a light came on inside of me and has stayed lit ever since. I keep the light aglow by using my conscious mind and free will to appreciate all that I have. I keep it bright by *choosing* to be happy. With that light lit, I have the lust for life and abundance of energy that I'd only dreamed of, before. It is mine now, and it will always be here for me, because I practice what I have learned through Grace.

I allow myself to feel all of my feelings without judgment. I prostrate when things get overwhelming. I live my life the way I want to, and on a daily basis, I do things that make me feel good and bring me joy.

It is a simple recipe, isn't it? Isn't that something you can imagine yourself following, too? When we push our feelings away, when we deny them, we are resisting them, and as I'm sure you've heard, *"What we resist persists!"*

When we feel great, we want that feeling to remain forever, and we resist any change that we think might bring us down. We believe there is a limit to the wonderful experiences we can have, so we cling to them, and try to extend them, not realizing we're actually bringing the end to the good feelings through those very actions!

Each moment and experience is a unique gift. Don't try and hold onto the "good" moments, and don't rush to be past the "bad". Free yourself from the habit of judging your experiences as good and bad. The Divine does not label events as positive or negative, good or bad, only humans do that. To the Divine, and to the Enlightened, everything is just an experience. There is no good or bad.

* * *

Grandma's Real World Example

A student of mine shared a powerful experience with me on this topic. Her grandson is at an age where he fusses a bit when he leaves his parents. She picked him up one day, and by the time she got him into the car seat, he was in total distress. Her habit was to try and make everything better, so she attempted to soothe him. He just got angrier! He looked up at her and yelled, *"Grandma, shut up!"*

Suddenly, it dawned on her that he was simply feeling his feelings, letting them flow. Her attempts to soothe him were stifling that natural flow. She decided to just let him be, and watch what happened.

For a little while, he made quiet sounds, squirming and shuffling around, moving the energy through him. In the blink of an eye his entire mood shifted and he was happy and giggling! I love this story. It showed my friend that Grandma doesn't need to make everything alright for everyone, she doesn't have to exhaust herself trying to fix everyone around her. She decided to set down that burden - and it was such a heavy one, too. She instantly felt lighter! Through this experience, she saw so clearly how we program children to not feel or express their emotions. We think that is helping, making them happier. But sometimes the most powerful thing we can do for another human being is to *just let them be.*

Gifts in Everything We Experience

No matter what happens to us or around us, no matter how troubling or negative it seems, there is a gift in it. Every one of our experiences helps us to learn more about who we are. Tragedy can spark latent talents we might not have known about otherwise. Seeming misfortune can set fire to passions that lead us to victories in our lives.

We live in a world of contrast: contrasts of what we like and dislike, contrasts between what we want more of, and what we do not want at all. Whenever we experience something, and realize we don't like it, and know that we don't want to experience it again, an equal and opposite desire ignites within us, a desire for what we *do* want.

The vibration of that new desire spreads out from us, and acts on the world around us. So once you have released your resistance to what you *don't* want, your new desires will already have been drawn to you! That's why there is always a gift to be found, no matter how bad things may seem.

Want some concrete examples? Ok!

I was drawn to the healing arts because of my anxiety and panic attacks. A dear friend of mine was lead to a healing path, because she had diabetes. I have met women who were badly abused, and through their experience, they were led to develop empowerment programs for other women, turning their experience into a victory. If we had not had the experiences of anxiety, of diabetes, of abuse, we would have never found ourselves on these paths that allow us to help others!

Our culture conditions us to have a victim consciousness, it teaches us to think of ourselves as victims. This view steals our power, and keeps us in a space where we are attracting more people, events and circumstances that victimize us.

If you have created a victimization story for yourself, consider changing the story. You may have collected a lot of evidence that you are a victim of circumstances or abusive people. Consider how you can exchange that evidence for a collection that reveals the hidden gifts of your experiences. Consider how you can change your perspective.

Changing your perspective is such a powerful tool - and the more empowering your perspective is, the closer it will carry you to Truth. (Truth is always empowering). No matter what we are facing, how dark and pointless an experience may seem, there is always a gift within it. Shift your focus to the gift; this change will allow you to create a life closer to your desires, instead of feeding the vibration of a victim-driven life.

There's an old Cherokee story that illustrates this nicely:

TWO WOLVES

One evening, an old Cherokee told his grandson about a battle that goes on inside people.

He said, "My son, the battle is between two wolves inside us all. One wolf is Evil; it is anger, envy, jealousy, sorrow, regret, greed, arrogance, self-pity, guilt, resentment, inferiority, lies, false pride, superiority, and ego. The other wolf is God; it is joy, peace, love, hope, serenity, humility, kindness, benevolence, empathy, generosity, truth, compassion and faith."

The grandson thought about this for a minute, then he asked his grandfather, "Which wolf wins?"

The old Cherokee answered, "The one we feed."

We Choose Our Perspective, Even in Pain

I have met many people who have tragically lost a loved one; each person has a different perspective on the experience of grief. Some have huge heart awakenings - they realize that only love is real, only love matters, that everything else (even death) is an illusion. Through the loss, they learn how important it is to shower the people closest to them with love, and this flowering of the heart springs from the illusion of loss.

Other people experience loss and they are ruined emotionally for life. They never truly emerge from their grief, remaining angry and bitter at the world, feeling mistreated and abused by life itself. They close down to love and to other people, and fall dead inside.

There is no judgment here - no right, or wrong way to deal with such a painful loss. But we have a choice. We always have a choice.

The question is which choice will bring the most empowerment, the most joy? It's a crucial question, and one we can each only answer for ourselves.

We are often very attached to our stories, attached to our pain and suffering, and we believe that our pain is unique and special. For some of us, that sense of "specialness" we have in our pain can outweigh the desire for peace and enlightenment.

But what happens if we look for the gift in our pain and troubles?

Let's Look at this Idea From a More Global Perspective...

Whenever a catastrophic event occurs in the world, there are tremendous gifts lying within the wreckage.

The BP oil spill in the Gulf of Mexico raised awareness in people of not only the importance of human life, but the impact of our lives on all life forms, and on the Earth, herself. Through this catastrophe, more people than ever recognized that we truly need to be the Stewards of the Earth that we came here to be. The oil spill showed us the interconnectedness of all things, helped us to recognize that we can no longer dump pollutants in one part of the world without it having catastrophic effects to *all* of the water systems of the planet. And people from all walks of life joined in to help along the coast, some of them people who had never even considered the benefits of serving the community before.   People came together, unified for the common good of all - that is a gift, born from a catastrophe.

Hurricane Katrina, the Tsunami in Asia, the world-wide reaction to 9-11, they each showed us that human compassion is immense! Hearts opened wide, people came together to help and serve.

Through these catastrophes, people awoke into Oneness, working together to heal; even in the face of the world's worst disasters, there are gifts.

If this works on a global scale, don't you think it might work on a personal scale, too? Don't you think it might work for you, in your own life?

No matter what you have been through, how hard it seems, there is a gift for you in that experience. Retrieve the gifts. Release the baggage. All of that pain you are clinging to? It is only the box and the wrapping for the gift. It is OK to let the wrapping go.

The Grace you are receiving through this book will help you enormously as you shift your perspective, and learn to receive the gifts. As you see the Truths behind even the darkest experiences, your vision of the world will brighten and clear.

Working with Relationships

When we interact with others, we rarely experience the Truth of who they really are. Instead, we form impressions, draw mental images of who we *think* they are. We label that image with words: sweet, bitchy, rude, critical, funny. It's that image of them that we interact with. We put people in boxes and then expect them to react according to our labels, positive or negative. The labels may have very little to do with who they really are, but it sets up our expectations, and lines up the vibration of our encounters.

Seeing others through the distorted lens of our impressions, we set our vibration to match that expectation. This leaves the people we interact with no room to just be who they are; we expect them to be a certain way, so they must deliver. Our own energy demands it! So when we expect the worst of someone, we create that reality. We put them in a box, and that box limits the ways we allow them to act and react around us.

If you want someone to act differently with you, *you must shift first.*

This probably goes against everything you have been conditioned to do. Your False Self is likely kicking up now, asking "Why do I have to change? They are the problem, not me!" But we create 100% of our reality, we set the energy of our interactions. We must take responsibility for our lives.

Remember what you've learned about acceptance and resistance in this book? It applies to the people you interact with, too. Wanting someone to be different is a form of resistance; it reinforces the very behaviors from them that you wish would change. Resistance creates suffering; it doesn't create change.

If you are having difficulty with a relationship, *you* must shift. You must begin to love and accept others for who they are, as they are. You must take responsibility for releasing your expectations of them and their behavior, because then, and only then, will they and the relationship be able to shift. *The more responsibility you claim, the more power you have.*

Let me give you a real life example: my friend Lisa's parents argue a lot, so Lisa resists spending much time with them. One day, she and her husband had plans with her parents, and as usual, they were dreading it. They knew how the day would play out - there would be a lot of hostility, turmoil and conflict. On the ride over, Lisa and her husband talked about their expectations, their past experiences, and how horrible the day was going to be.

Can you see how they lined up the vibration of their encounter with Lisa's parents? By discussing the fights, expecting the arguing, and fueling their expectations by speaking about the past, they were creating a repeat of those experiences. They were speaking it into existence.

When they got to Lisa's parents' house, there was indeed a lot of fighting. Lisa and her husband just shook their heads, seeing the experience as their evidence that "They are just that way, always fighting!"

But as Lisa and her husband got ready to leave, her mother spoke up. "I am so sorry we fought today," she said. "It is weird, because we have been getting along really well lately." A light went on within Lisa; she realized how much *their* expectations had to do with creating the problem.

* * *

Changing the Focus

After that day, Lisa and her husband consciously chose to make a change *within themselves*. They dropped all of their grudges and expectations based on past history, and deliberately focused on everything they loved, enjoyed and appreciated about Lisa's parents. The next time the four of them got together, they had a delightful time!

When we focus on what we don't like about someone, we bring that out in our interactions with them. If you want to experience more of what you love about a person, focus on all that you appreciate about them. Look for the gifts and blessings in your interactions with others. Drop your resistance, create a space of acceptance, shift your perspective.

People reflect what you expect of them. Change what you expect, and your experience of them will change, too.

About Your Worthiness

Know this: You are worthy. You are loved, and you are worthy of love. You've been given a body - *this proves your worthiness*. Each breath you take is evidence that you are worthy!

Only humans have doubts about our worth - other sentient beings are not plagued with these feelings and concerns. The idea that we are unworthy is a huge lie, created in the mind, and that's why it feels so terrible - we are lying to ourselves! Our human perceptions about worth are usually far from the Truth.

When you think a thought that is not true, that thought triggers a negative emotion, a bad feeling. That bad feeling is a signal that the Source is not in agreement with your thought. Your untrue thought is disconnecting you from Source, creating distance between you and the Divine. Being disconnected from Source is supposed to feel bad - it tells us when we're moving away from Truth.

And the Truth is this: The Presence loves everyone equally, no matter what. Nothing you do can change the Divine's love for you. Nothing you do, or don't do, can make the Source love you any more or any less. The Divine loves, cherishes and adores you exactly the way that you are. You do not have to be, say or do anything to receive this love. You do not have to earn it. The love of the Infinite is freely given; it cannot be lost or taken back.

Some of us have trouble accepting this love. We have been conditioned to believe we must work hard, suffer, toil and earn the good things in life, but this is not true. We are worthy, and we are loved beyond our wildest imaginings, without having to do a single thing!

Part of Enlightenment is learning to love all people and all things the same way that the Presence does; this flowering of the heart is an amazing feeling. As the process progresses, our conditioned judgments are replaced with an unconditional love for all people. Gone are our criticisms, skepticism, our envy, jealousy, and need to compete, replaced by acceptance and love.

This doesn't mean that we condone behavior that is not life supportive; it means that we see *beyond* the behavior. People are not their behavior. Most of us have been conditioned to behave in negative ways, ways that do not support Truth. We can learn to behave in more positive, life-affirming ways. We are all growing, expanding, opening and evolving every day, so it is important to love the truth of who we are.

Don't limit your love with judgments and labels based purely on behavior. Behavior changes. Truth doesn't.

When you find yourself judging others or yourself, remember that judgment is just an ingrained habit. As you become aware of that habit, you can change it. Recognize it for what it is, choose consciously to love and accept the person as they are. Exercise your free will; choose to forgive yourself for judging. These choices bring freedom.

If there are people in your life who are abusive, and it does not feel good to be around them, don't!

Stepping beyond judgment and into unconditional love in no way implies that we must tolerate abuse or accept hurtful behavior. This is about loving our brothers and sisters in this world, to the very best of our ability. We're not required to stay in situations that are not beneficial to us.

When you live from a place of acceptance and love, there is no good, bad or evil - there is simply conditioning, patterning and predispositions.

People are not their patterning and conditioning, but if they're choosing to behave in ways that are hurtful you don't have to put up with it. Distinguish between the person and the pattern of behavior, love the truth of them, but of course you don't have to endure hurtful behavior. It's OK to love from a safe distance!

You Are Worthy!

You are worthy of beautiful relationships, prosperity, wealth, health and life. The Infinite loves the person who is nice and kind, and the Infinite loves the ax murderer. Right here, right now, know and accept that you are worthy. Owning your worth allows you to open, flower and expand in miraculous ways.

The Divine is constantly giving you Blessings; your gift back to the Divine is to receive the Blessings. Feelings of unworthiness do not fulfill this gift to the Presence. So deem yourself worthy! Grace will help you accept this gift.

Life is about joy, bliss, creating, expanding, living and having fun. You hold the key within you about what you attract into your life through vibration; you get to create and choose whatever you want.

Life is your buffet, absolutely *everything* is available.

I want you to pause, and really feel the Truth of that statement. *Absolutely everything is available.* It is true! Our bodies love to hear the Truth; the Truth liberates and sets us free. Organized religion has perpetrated shame, guilt and fear. It has taught many of us to believe we are unworthy. In Church, before people receive "God in word" and the Sacrament during Mass, they must first ask for mercy and forgiveness. Before receiving the Eucharist they must plead, "Lord, though I am not worthy to receive You, only say the word and I shall be healed."

People say these words over and over, programming and demeaning themselves through the words they are speaking. They are teaching themselves that they are unworthy! Entire social systems are built on this false idea. We are programmed that we are wicked and naughty. We are taught that we need to plead for forgiveness.

But the Divine does not judge or criticize our thoughts, words and actions; humans alone do that. There is no need to ask the Divine for forgiveness, because the Divine does not judge.

The Divine can be compared to a loving video camera, just observing and experiencing everything that is happening, putting no labels or judgments on anything. Try this as an exercise; practice being a video camera for a day. Simply observe your life as a video camera would, with no labels, no judgment, taking everything in simply as an experience. You may find this practice is very liberating.

If you are carrying any feelings or labels of shame, guilt, unworthiness, drop them now.

Befriend Your Mind

Remember that if an emotion feels bad, that feeling bad is letting you know that the Divine is not in agreement with the *thoughts* that are creating that bad feeling. The Divine is always in love and bliss. Unworthiness, shame, and guilt all feel bad because those feelings let you know that you are separate from Source.

If you are experiencing painful memories or negative thoughts, know they are just the Infinite's way of showing you where you need to forgive yourself, forgive someone else, or where you can look to reclaim more of your own personal power through shifting a limiting belief.

Negative feelings show us where there are hidden beliefs that are vibrating within us, consciously or unconsciously creating in our reality. They are helpful information! We want to know what may be lurking beneath the surface, creating negatives in our lives.

When a negative thought comes up, or a painful memory, say *"Yes!"* to it, welcome it, be open to it. It is trying to help you! By accepting and embracing those feelings, we stop being in conflict with the mind, and we can make friends with it. The mind is trying to help you always. There is no battle to win. By making you uncomfortable, the mind is simply showing you where you are not in alignment with Truth and your Divine self.

We hold onto painful memories. We have beliefs that do not serve us, we cling to fears and worries. The mind will bring these up to your conscious awareness for you to recognize, so that you can shift them into a more empowering perspective or belief.

Negative thoughts arise so they can illuminate your need to forgive yourself or someone else. Accepting those feelings and offering that forgiveness, allows you to reclaim vast amounts of your own personal power and get back into alignment with your Authentic, Divine self.

Your mind, the Universe, the Divine, they all have your back, because you are loved!

Focus on YOU First

Many spiritual people (and women in particular) give, give, give of themselves. We give so much that our personal cups of energy and resources are drained, and there is nothing left but fumes. Still, we keep giving even those last drops.

This is not life supportive or healthy. As flight attendants tell us on airplanes, "Place the mask over your own face *first;* only then help the person next to you."

Even in life, we must tend to our own needs first. We must fill our own cup with abundance until it overflows; only then we can give that overflow to others. When our own growth has progressed, we can hold our vibration high in the face of whatever happens around us. That puts us in the best possible place to assist others.

As you process the information in this book, please focus solely on yourself. Once you are stabilized, then you can help others. For now, help yourself. Soothe yourself. Be soft with yourself. Love and cherish yourself.

In this moment, make peace with wherever you are. Know that you have done the very best you could given the tools and knowledge you have had.

When people know better, they do better. And you are learning! You are growing, expanding and awakening to who you really are, more and more each day. This means that you, too, will do better as you move forward. Enjoy the journey. There is no rush to get anywhere. Enjoy the unfolding.

Where There Is Light, There Cannot Be Darkness

With each Grace Blessing, the Divine Light is shining into all aspects of your being. Everything within you is being illuminated. Stagnant energies from past hurts, traumas and experiences are being exposed to the light, so they can be resolved fully, finally. When these energies remain trapped in the body, unmoving and stagnant, they can cause disease later on. They need to move.

You may feel these energies as they move up in vibrations and out of your life. The experience can be intense and sometimes uncomfortable. If you remember to let go, to practice acceptance and just let the feelings be, without fighting them, they will be transformed. All you have to do is allow the feelings and energy to flow. If you let this happen, you will experience a tremendous feeling of lightness and freedom. The empowerment at the end of this is priceless beyond words.

Any discomfort you feel means the energy is finally moving! You want this to happen, so welcome the discomfort!

You can help these old emotions and energies to move along. Try any (or all!) of the practices below:

- Sit in silence; practice deep breathing, and allow yourself to fully feel the pure essence and energy of the emotion.

- Break the silence! Scream, yell it out, let out everything you want to say. (This is a private exercise, not to be done in front of or directed at anyone)

- Beat up your pillows, beat things with your pillows, (Again, this is to be done in private).

- Write a letter, pour out everything you need to say onto the page, get the feelings out of you! When you've finished, without showing it to anyone, destroy the letter and finish releasing the energy.

- Dance wildly to music you love. Dance wildly to music you hate. Dance!

- Exercise, get moving! Any kind of physical activity that you enjoy moves energy.

These actions all move energy. As your body moves, as your mind moves, the energy moves, freeing your life to move in new, different, positive ways.

More Illumination for You:

People can harm your physical body, but no one can hurt your mind and emotions, because they are not solid! The meaning you give to the experience, the meaning that you yourself assign is what causes you such psychological pain. You are in control of this. You can choose to view things with different meanings, different perspectives.

No one has the power to truly hurt you. Others can hurt your body, but physical pain only lasts so long. The meanings you give the events in your life are what really hurts, what really lasts. Take responsibility for this. Own it.

Take *ALL* of your power back, now.

Mastery of Mind and Emotions

Being human, we have emotions that we don't like to experience. We probably even have some emotions that we refuse to feel at all, especially if we grew up with families who taught us to repress them. But if we truly want to be free, we must learn to allow any and all emotions to flow through us without resistance.

A little later in this section, you'll find a guided exercise to help you process whatever feelings may arise in your journey; it will help you learn to experience your emotions in a gentle and easy way.

Please be tremendously compassionate and forgiving of yourself through this experience.

Even though I will ask you to intensify uncomfortable feelings, this process is not about increasing your suffering. So approach the process gently, treating both the emotions and yourself with tremendous love, openness and compassion.

We often give feelings and emotions way too much power over us because we misunderstand what emotion really is. There are no such things as "bad" emotions! An emotion is simply energy that wants to move. If we pay attention, we can locate that energy within our bodies, experience it fully, and gently help it to move. This small awareness is one of the first steps in becoming fully aware and self nurturing.

Know this: *Any feeling fully felt rises in vibration and dissolves.*

Be gentle with your feelings, accept them without resistance. When you stop being hard on yourself, when you stop criticizing and judging yourself for having emotions, you will find your freedom from emotions.

You don't need to judge feelings as good or bad - emotions aren't either one. They're just Divine energy at various vibratory rates.

The Divine is always in love and bliss, and that is what it ultimately wants to express. When we feel anything other than love and bliss, we have temporarily forgotten the Truth of who we are. To get back in alignment with the Truth, we can simply acknowledge what we are feeling, feel it fully, let it flow on through. When we do that, the discomfort dissolves. Simple, isn't it?

I call this "feeling into the feeling", and you can do it with any emotion. This is not just for lower vibrational emotion, it is for *all* emotions. Feeling into positive emotions can take us even higher into ecstasy! Learn to accept and welcome everything you feel, and you will be free forever.

Just like every other part of this journey, there is no deadline for when you are supposed to release any particular feeling. If you've gone through this process and you still don't feel neutral, don't worry. You may have to "feel into" a particular emotion several times, until the energy dissolves or you've moved into more peaceful feelings. Don't judge your progress on this process. Be easy, kind and gentle on yourself and let it take as long as it takes.

Let go, let Grace help you with this. All we need to do is release resistance; then everything flows easily and naturally.

* * *

Tips for Feeling Into Your Emotions

As you do the exercise, lay down comfortably, or snuggle into your favorite chair with your eyes closed. Being physically comfortable will help you be more gentle with yourself and your emotions.

Set your intention as you begin. Tell yourself, "This is going to be *easy,* it will *reduce* pain and suffering."

Bring one feeling at a time into the process. If you find that through this process one feeling flows into another naturally, it's OK to allow and follow that flow, but don't try to tackle too much at once.

The power and freedom of this process is *purely in feeling*. Anytime you start to think about the *story* around the feeling, let it go. Let go of the circumstances that created the feeling, let go of how right you are and how wrong others are, let go of what you see as the facts. This is about pure *feeling*.

If you're struggling with thoughts of blame, ask yourself "Do you want to be right or do you want to be happy?" No one else matters in this process, no one else's part in the hurt or discomfort you feel is relevant for this exercise. You are the only person you need to think about in this process, you are the only one that matters.

Get ready to enjoy this practice! Imagine saying "Yes!" to this experience, saying "Yes!" to yourself and to your feelings. Imagine approaching it with joy! Coming to your feelings from a positive, loving, peaceful place will help them move and flow through you.

As you practice this method over time, it will become instinctual for you to allow all feelings and emotions to flow. Remember that emotions are energy that want to move; they are no big deal. This way of thinking will become natural for you as you move forward.

At the end of the exercise, there is a Grace Blessing waiting for you, ready to assist you in the full resolution of whatever emotions you are feeling. All the help, strength and wisdom you need is within you, and you have Grace on your side, too! Once you learn to feel into your feelings, you will be able to be with any emotion, flow any emotion and you will become unsinkable!

How to "Feel into a Feeling"

Ready to get started?

As you begin, ask the Divine Presence to help and assist you. Ask that this process be gentle, elegant and graceful, and know that it will be! You are the author, director and creator of your reality; you get to decide how this goes for you.

Now make yourself comfortable. Close your eyes. Notice how you feel in this moment, in this *now* moment. Whatever emotion you are experiencing, right now, bring it into this exercise.

Locate the energy of the emotion in your body, feel around for where it is centered, and observe it there. Observe like a camera, without assigning meaning or value to what you are experiencing; just let the feeling exist. When you've located the emotion in your body, place your awareness there. Feel it.

If the feeling is uncomfortable or startling, if it comes with odd or scary sensations, know that it is just a feeling, just sensation, just energy. Emotion cannot hurt you. You are not a victim of emotion, you are an observer of it.

As you observe the feeling, welcome it! Embrace it fully. Ask the emotion to intensify itself. You can ask out-loud, if you wish.

Acknowledge that this feeling is here for a reason; it has something powerful to teach you about yourself. It is trying to show you where you have a false belief, where you need to forgive. This emotion is trying to show you places you can *reclaim more of your personal power*, to get back in alignment with your Divine self.

Notice all sensations, symptoms and feelings. Ask these sensations to intensify as much as they can. If you are feeling fear, speak to the fear, tell it "Give me everything you've got! " If you've been hiding from your feeling, tell it "I am sorry I have been ignoring you and running from you. I am right here, and you have my full attention now. Give me everything you've got!"

Don't be surprised if one emotion turns into another. They shift and change as the vibration changes. Go with it until the feeling rises up in vibration and shifts to a good feeling. Stay with this for as long as it takes, welcoming and intensifying each shift.

Give the emotion all the energy and space it needs to move.

As the feeling shifts and changes, celebrate its movement, celebrate that an old unwanted emotion is moving and leaving. Whether you were aware of this emotion or not, its energy was affecting your reality.

Tell it that it is welcome back anytime. This step is important! It takes any resistance off of feeling the feeling, so make sure to welcome the feeling back whenever it wishes to pay you a visit again.

Remember: any emotion fully felt moves up in vibration. This is the natural movement of energy. This is what it wants to do. Trust in the elegance and simplicity of this process, and you'll get to a place where you welcome all emotions. This is emotional freedom!

Your Next Grace Blessing

Please gaze at the artwork for a couple of minutes. Then close your eyes and rest for fifteen minutes or longer, allowing the Divine to do the work *for* you. Notice, experience, feel and allow. Know how profoundly loved, cherished and supported you are. Receive, receive, receive. You are LOVED. You ARE LOVE.

Additional Resource: *If you find yourself struggling and strongly resistant to your emotions, you may find the "Mastery of Mind and Emotions" audio program useful. The guided process walks you through feeling and being with any and all emotion. The Grace that flows through the audio does most of the work for you and the program culminates with a Grace Blessing at the end. It is a simple yet powerful process that many have found very helpful in their unfolding. It is available at: http://shop.ericarock.com/mastery-of-mind-and-emotions/*

Drop the Drama

When things happen in our lives that elicit negative feelings and lower vibrations, remember that emotion is not good or bad; it is all just information. Uncomfortable feelings let us know where we have blind spots in our lives, places where our life-energy is not flowing freely. We need this information, so having it is a good thing.

After a Grace Blessing, if something happens that does not feel good, just be with it and it will pass. When we *resist* what is happening, make it wrong and judge ourselves for it? It causes suffering. With Grace Blessings, life will bring whatever you need to experience to become whole. You do not need to go and dig around for things to fix, heal or clear. Those days are over!

Whatever happens through your day, just *feel* through it. If a house mate yells at you, if you have a conflict with a co-worker, or a familial dispute, experience it. Let it be what it is. If it makes you angry, feel the anger; if it makes you sad, feel that too. Feel everything as it arises and it will move.

* * *

Remember How You Were When You Were Little

Children are our greatest teachers. They feel worthy, they let energy flow freely, they authentically feel all of their emotions. One second they are crying, the next screaming, then suddenly they are giggling. They do not hold grudges, judge or criticize. Children know how to just "be", so be like them!

This is not a mind thing. We don't need to speak about it or think about it, we only need to *feel* it. When we relax and let the emotion flow through us, the energy doesn't stick; it moves through us naturally. But if we stop the flow of energy to think about it, when we pause to gossip or judge the people involved, we get mired in the emotion, tangled up in the story we create around it. The stories and criticisms we use to label events make us feel bad.

A woman I know would say, "Drop the story, feel the feeling." I couldn't agree more! As your unfolding deepens, feeling good will become more important to you than being right. Being happy will be more important than making others wrong. The stories won't matter. Spinning dramas around our experience casts us as victims and villains. It doesn't solve anything, it is not productive, life supportive or empowering; it will not bring you the life you want. *The degree to which you judge is the degree to which you do not "get it".*

Drop the drama habit now. Grace Blessings will help you create a drama free life. Practice awareness. Practice noticing. Practice feeling. Be willing to put up with paradoxes in this book. Again, what is "true" at one level of consciousness is not necessarily "true" at another.

Resolving Conflict

Most conflicts and troubles we have in our relationships are due to *misunderstanding.* So seek to understand more. Strive to avoid assumptions. Don't take anything personally.

When people are happy and have enough resources, they will always be generous and kind. Everything negative that someone does is trying to *meet a need.* If we can find out what that need is, we can help them to meet it more positively.

When we recognize that negative behaviors are based in need, we realize that the behaviors are worthy of *empathy*, not judgment. There are no bad or evil actions, only non-life-supportive programming. When you fully grasp this truth (and you will!) You'll discover that judgment will just dissolve.

Setting relationships right is key to your spiritual liberation and freedom.

We are each 100% responsible for the quality of our lives. We've been taught by our culture to play the blame game, but there is no place for blame in self actualization and enlightenment. Who is right and who is wrong, who is at fault, who is to blame, who cares! Those questions don't matter. The key question to ask is "What can I do about it?"

Think about this: *The amount of responsibility you take equals the amount of power you claim.* Take responsibility for your experience. Drop the desire for other people to behave differently, and take the responsibility for change onto yourself. Don't place your personal happiness on anything outside of your control - it only sets you up for suffering.

Empowerment comes from within. Every change, internal or external, comes from within. Know that "the world is as you are." The world will transform as you transform!

* * *

What to Do when You're Upset

If you find yourself upset with someone, go within. Feel into the emotions, let the energy shift and raise in vibration before you speak or act. You may discover that once you've felt through everything, you don't even need to say a word! It's so nice to save that time and energy.

When my own emotional vibration is low, I won't speak to anyone or make any important decisions. I wait it out, feel through it, and then act from a place of neutrality and great power.

So even when it seems as though someone is intentionally causing a problem for you, stay within, keep your power inside, feel the emotions and let the energy resolve and flow. When you are clear, you can address the problem if you still feel the need.

Once you've lifted your own vibration, you'll be able to deal with the situations from a centered place of kindness, approaching it in a way that will elicit openness from the other party. Ask yourself, "What do I want in this moment?" and then choose speech that is in alignment with what you want. You'll need to practice this; it's probably something you've never been taught to do. Be gentle and easy with yourself as you practice. This sort of loving communication is vital for the unfolding process, and crucial for our relationships - learn it gently!

* * *

Why I Stress Relationships

Everything in life is a relationship. We have a relationship to ourselves, co-workers, family, friends, to the Divine, to the Earth and ALL life. We want clean, harmonious, balanced and peaceful relationships; we want the feelings in our relationships to lift us and help us maintain happiness.

Sometimes that desire tempts us to censor our feelings. But emotions cannot be transcended, stuffed down, escaped from, deleted, fixed, healed or cleared; they must be *felt and experienced*. Emotions are a natural part of being human and being alive! Rejoice and celebrate them.

Part of the enlightenment process is embracing our humanness, so welcome to the human race! Embrace the totality of your being. Accept all parts of you, resist nothing.

As the Divine awakens within you, you realize at the level of the heart that we are all One, and that existence is all one giant relationship. With this realization, the perceptions of scarcity, danger, competition, shift and dissolve. Because we are One with everything and everyone, there is never anything to fear. When we all reach this realization, we no longer want to harm anyone else, because we know we are only hurting ourselves.

This is the start of beautiful, peaceful relationships. Once the majority of people are enlightened, all of our personal, communal and global issues will resolve from an entirely new consciousness, an awareness that sees all of the unlimited possibilities and probabilities. Again, problems cannot be solved from the same consciousness which created them; awakening brings a radical new consciousness, and with it, radical new solutions to all of the issues we are facing. Isn't it an exciting perspective?

World peace will happen when we have attained peace within ourselves, the outer reflecting the inner.

Additional Resource: If you'd like more tips on loving, open communication, The Center for Non Violent Communication (http://www.cnvc.org) is a wonderful resource.

Misperceptions Cause Suffering

Potentially uncomfortable circumstances and events occur in everyone's life. Depending on your perception, they can bring you pain and suffering, or happiness and joy. It's your choice. Your experience depends on the story you choose to tell yourself about what is happening.

Your free will, your ability to consciously *choose* your story is a gift from the Divine; it's a gift that can make a huge impact in your life. The perceptions you choose make the difference between hurt and happiness - these choices explain why one person can be troubled and hurt by a particular circumstance, and another person in the same situation is not bothered at all. It's all in how you look at it.

Everyone, universally, wants to be happy, and holding perceptions that bring you pain is just not helpful. Telling stories about the hurt won't give you a beautiful happy life.

Truth Never Hurts.

That's so important that I want to say it again: *Truth never hurts.*

Truth, with a capital "T", is another word for God, the Presence, the Divine. Truth is the most powerful perception you can have; the closer to Truth your perceptions are, the more empowered you will be.

Ask yourself, "What perception can I have about this event will bring *me* the most empowerment"? Listen carefully for the answer. The perception that brings you the most empowerment will be the closest to the Truth.

We lie to ourselves all the time, tell ourselves disempowering stories that weaken us and take us further from Truth. So use your free will, use your conscious mind to look upon events through the eyes of the Infinite, through the eyes of Truth. You will never, ever, feel like a victim again. The Truth will set you free!

"It's all in how you look at it." If you engage this teaching into your day to day reality, if you practice this every day, you will change your life.

* * *

Seek to Understand the Behavior of Others

Try to put yourself in their shoes, see the situation through their eyes. What if you were the "other person", what if you were brought up with their parents? What if you had their conditioning and predispositions, and were shaped by the same experiences that they've had? You would behave the *exact* same way they do!

This is part of why we have no right to judge, ever.

When you catch yourself judging someone else, know that it is only because you do not fully understand. And when you feel that someone is judging *you* unfairly, know that they do not fully understand. When there is understanding, there is no judgment.

If you pay attention to relationships and study what happens in them, you will discover that at the heart of every upset, fight or disagreement is a misunderstanding. Strive to *understand,* and you'll be freed from so much upset and trouble!

Do this, and you will become more compassionate, automatically, without effort.

About Judgment

When we were first born, we were innocents, in the Garden of Eden. As infants, we didn't judge ourselves or others. We simply lived, free. We loved our fat naked bodies!

But as we grew, we learned judgment from our families, from our schoolmates, from our teachers. We learned to think in terms of good, bad, right, wrong. We learned to judge ourselves, to judge others. We learned to constantly worry about other people's judgments of us.

Grown, we are in a living hell; we are in judgment. We are no longer free.

We wear masks, put on facades. We do not act as our genuine or authentic selves. We suffer, we feel cut off from life, cut off from the Source, cut off from ourselves and each other - all because we imagine we must avoid being judged.

Just reading this *feels* bad doesn't it? Notice how you *feel* here!

* * *

A Real Life Example of Judgment, Stories and Perception

Once, at a fire-walking event I attended with a friend, the facilitator had a picture of the Hindu deity Ganesha mounted on a board. During her talk, the facilitator casually moved the board out of her way, placing it flat on the floor, so that Ganesha's image was face down. My friend was shocked and offended, so angered that he left the room. He didn't even finish the workshop.

The next morning, I asked him where he went. His entire demeanor changed! He started clenching his fists. His breath became shallow and fast, his eyes narrowed; you could practically feel the adrenaline coursing through his body. His voice was angry as he explained how upset he was about this facilitator, how disrespectfully she had treated Ganesha. He ranted and raved for a few minutes, and I listened.

Now from my perspective, I didn't see things like that at all. I wanted to laugh. I couldn't help thinking "Do you really believe that Ganesha was offended, and judged the facilitator's actions? Of course not!"

All of the disrespect, all of the judgment was in his filters, his personal perspective. He had gotten terribly upset in response to the story *he alone created* about the event. The event in and of itself had no power to create this response in him.

He could have changed the story, chosen to see the event differently, and not been upset at all!

Think about this story, and apply it in your life. How often do we do this to ourselves? How many times do we go to the bank, grocery store, deli, the movie theater, and people are less than polite to us? How often do we perceive them as offensive, how often do we tell ourselves stories about how rude they are, how they've wronged us?

These day to day events can send us reeling for hours, sometimes ruining our entire day. But do we really want to be like that? Do we really want to be like puppets, allowing the people, events and outer circumstances of life to have this kind of power over us? I don't, and if you're reading this book, you probably don't, either! So take your power back; no one and nothing has the power to create anything in your life, bad or good, unless you allow it.

You are one hundred percent responsible for your life. That responsibility can be a big pill to swallow, but it is true. Once you can accept it, once you can operate from that place of responsibility, you are beginning to truly step into your mastery. As you step into that responsibility, you begin to create the life that you truly want to have.

In each moment of our life, we have a choice: to be empowered, or to be a victim. To be happy, or unhappy. The choice is always yours.

What are you going to choose? What do you choose in *this* moment?

Setting Relationships Right:
Peacemaking & Forgiveness

Forgiveness is a powerful, but often misunderstood healing practice. Forgiveness isn't just about other people - it's about us! All forgiveness is self-forgiveness; we are One on this planet, all interconnected. We cannot spill oil in one part of the ocean without it affecting all of the waters. We cannot hurt another person without hurting ourselves.

We must awaken into this awareness, this Oneness. Setting all of your relationships right is key to your liberation and happiness; forgiveness is part of this. Offering forgiveness doesn't mean that the harm someone else did is acceptable behavior, it just means that you love yourself enough to let the harm go, to free yourself from the pain and burden you are carrying.

What I am about to say is really important, so please pay attention: *The Divine does not forgive.*

When we see everything through the eyes of Truth, through the eyes of the Divine, we realize that there really isn't anything to forgive at all. Where there is no judgment, there is nothing wrong. The Divine does not forgive, because there *is nothing to forgive.* This understanding of forgiveness is an advanced way of feeling, seeing and being; the prayers that follow will help you reach that understanding, and take another step in Enlightenment.

About "The Gift of Life Prayers"

A dear teacher of mine, Howard Wills, does all of his healing work through peacemaking and forgiveness. With his permission, I am reprinting his Gift of Life prayers, affirmations and explanations. You can find the originals on his website, www.howardwills.com. These prayers are extremely effective and freeing. Praying them expands your consciousness, and will help release you from the resentments, physical pain and burdens that you carry. If you are finding yourself feeling low, angry, overly critical or life just seems hard, please use them!

I am including them in The TRUE You for a number of reasons. One reason is that these prayers were an *instrumental* part of my own personal enlightenment and awakening process. They are a big part of *how* I got where I AM today. Another reason for sharing is that they will help you clean up your relationships and set them right - a significant aspect of this Awakening process!

Sharing these prayers with hundreds of clients and watching their over-the-top transformation has gladdened my heart in ways that there are no words to describe!

* * *

Hints and Tips

When you first work with the Gift of Life prayers, you may feel as though you are just reading words off a page. Keep practicing, speaking them aloud. Spend time with them, and you will begin to have deeper and deeper experiences. Many people find that in the middle of reading these prayers, they have physical sensations and releases. It's quite an experience! So practice. You *will* feel relief, you will get results and have a more beautiful harmonious life. As Howard says, "Healing is a feeling!"

Approach the prayers with an attitude of joy and happiness. You are helping yourself and the people you love to be free. These prayers of forgiveness free all of your relationships, past and present. They free your spouse, your family members and all of your ancestors, back through all time and space. Everyone receives the benefits.

I once had a very interesting experience with this; I was doing the prayers in my car, listening to the CD I have of them. As I prayed, I observed that my car was filled with many of my deceased relatives, with a bright light around each of them. Tears of gratitude streaming down their faces, and I knew they were showing me appreciation for doing the prayers! I realized the great power contained within the Gift of Life Prayers - as we do them here in this life, it helps those on the other side of life, as well.

Each and every one of us carries the culmination of all of the thoughts, words and deeds of our ancestors. Each family has certain patterns, passed down through the generations. But having those patterns doesn't mean you are trapped in them. Being predisposed to something does not mean you are stuck with it! You can dissipate the negative predispositions that you have inherited, and free yourself, family members and your ancestors. You can develop a more positive disposition, choosing and creating a more positive reality for yourself through your thoughts, words and actions. The Grace that you are receiving assists with these changes immensely. You have so much help and support through the energy of the Blessings!

You'll notice that Howard uses the word Lord in his forgiveness prayers. If this does not resonate with you, please refer to the Infinite in any way you choose. But if you can use the word Lord comfortably, please do use it! "Lord" has been used for time eternal as a way to reference our Creator. Those years of use have created a powerful field of resonance around the word, making it very effective. Lord is not an exclusively masculine term; understood properly, it is a neutral word for the Creator and *does* include the feminine qualities of the Divine as well as the male.

Don't go into prayer with your tail between your legs, full of shame and guilt, and don't pray because of a sense of obligation, or because you think you should. Practice these prayers joyfully, empowered with the knowledge that there is something that you can do to make things right, something that you can do to make things better. *Pray from a place of power!* Enjoy the prayers and see your relationships flower and bloom. Give yourself a gift by speaking the entire system of prayers at least once, out loud. This will help to "install" them into your body, mind and spirit.

Speak them as often as you feel necessary. I did the entire of system of prayers every single day for at least a year, and I gained so much from taking the time for this practice. If you cannot do the full system, please do the ancestral prayer every single day. There truly is a magical chemistry created with these prayers. I do indeed hope you find them as valuable and useful as I do.

"Healing Is a Feeling" by Howard Wills

Have you ever heard someone say, "I'm feeling great," or "I'm feeling bad"? Pay attention to the words - they are correctly spoken, pointing directly to a feeling they are experiencing in their bodies. We humans, like all life forms, are a feeling. Yes, we are intellectual and even spiritual, but we are also feeling.

The human organism is immediately complicated with all the hundreds of body parts, bones, muscles, blood vessels, etc., not to mention the integration of the mind and feelings, and then our relationship to ourselves, others and the rest of creation. And yet with all this complexity, when we boil it all down, everything comes back to how we are feeling. Truthfully and honestly, are we feeling good or are we feeling bad?

There is an old saying, "We cannot lie to ourselves. We can lie to the rest of the world and they may not know it, but we can never lie to ourselves." And this brings us back to our feelings. If we are lying to others and/or trying to make excuses for our wrong actions, or trying to skirt issues or lie to ourselves about anything, we will begin to feel bad, inside and out - physically, mentally, emotionally and spiritually. The simple action of speaking the truth about anything or even everything creates freedom - no weight, no burden, no pain, and no lie. Speaking the truth is a powerful remedy to stress and pain. It relieves and releases burdens and makes complete freedom available to us now. When someone asks you a question, give him or her the truth. When you ask yourself a question, give yourself the truth. It is a powerful medicine that creates freedom, inner and outer healing, and a good healthy feeling. Healing is definitely a feeling, and speaking truthfully is a major action in creating inner and outer healing.

The native priests of Hawaii, called Kahunas, say those thoughts are physical, alive and have substance, even though they are invisible.

Thoughts are powerful and thoughts influence feelings. If we have negative, harmful, hurtful or hateful thoughts, we are creating the same types of negative feelings. So very simply, the remedy is to think positive, blessing, non-judgmental thoughts - simple, happy, positive thoughts. When we allow our thoughts to be simple positive and blessing, we free ourselves of the weight, burden and unhappiness created by negative judgmental thoughts. When we practice the art of positive, happy, non-judgmental thinking, we start feeling good, happy and free. When we start feeling good, happy, and free, our body and the health of our body will follow.

Remember, healing is a feeling, and if we are honestly feeling good inside and out, then our health will be a reflective measure of our true inner feelings, in a physical way. The inner feelings are reflected in our body just like our body reflects our inner feelings. To read the feelings is to read the body - to read the body is to read the feelings. Thoughts are real and are reflected physically through our bodies, our posture, our paths, and our illnesses. Let us think positive, blessing thoughts and create inner and outer healing for ourselves.

The last thing we can talk about that affects healing is the actions we and others take in life, the actions whereby others affect us, whereby we affect others, and whereby we affect ourselves. Action is the last leg of the triune creation process: thoughts, words, and deeds - to create the present and the future. In that healing is a feeling, our actions should be positive and a blessing to all concerned, including ourselves. By partaking in positive and blessing actions, we are creating blessings for everyone in our presence - and what we do to others, we do to ourselves. So by blessing others through positive actions, we are also blessing ourselves and helping ourselves to feel better.

There's nothing better than feeling good and nothing worse than feeling bad. Love yourself, be good to yourself, others, the earth and the life of the earth, and remember - HEALING IS A FEELING!

"Practice To Natural Healing" By Howard Wills:

- Deep Breathe - All Day, Every Day, Fresh Air - In On The Count of 8, Hold For The Count Of 8, And Out On The Count Of 8

- Listen To Your Inner Concerns And Settle All Dilemmas, Thus Creating Freedom

- Listen To Your Inner Voice And Always Do The Things You Know Are Right For You In Life

- Build A Relationship Of Love, Trust And Respect Between Your Inner And Outer Voice - Your Heart/Feelings And Your Mind. Become Your Own Best Friend - Mind To Heart/Feelings And Heart/Feelings To Mind ... Reward Yourself - Love Yourself - You Are Worthy

- Let All Your Thoughts, Words And Deeds Be Positive And Blessing

- Practice Humility, Gratitude, Love, Non-judgment, Patience, Compassion, Joy, And Happiness Through Continual Peacemaking In Life.

- Love, Accept And Respect All Things And All Situations In Life ... They Are Especially Designed For Your Personal Learning

- Eat Healthy, Living Foods As Much As Possible

- Enjoy And Appreciate The Gift Of Life

"Gift of Life Prayers and Affirmations" By Howard Wills

This information is to further your inner and outer development, encourage humility, heightened awareness, and healing through forgiveness, release, and peacemaking.

The more serious our life problems, whether physical or other, the more often the Prayers and Affirmations should be spoken. Speak these prayers and affirmations once or twice a day for transformation and spiritual growth; three to five times a day or more to address more serious or life threatening problems.

Deep breathe fresh air 3-5 minutes before speaking the prayers, and 3-5 minutes after. Whenever possible, face the sun, look toward the sun, close your eyes, and open your hands so that the light of the sun is on your palms. Begin to deep breathe long slow deep breaths, drawing in the fresh air and the light of the sun into your body through your eyes and palms. Breathe in on the count of eight, hold for the count of eight, and breathe out on the count of eight. Continue to hold the light within as you exhale. Fill yourself with the light as you breathe, charging yourself as if you are a solar battery.

The Prayers and Affirmations are Divinely inspired and have been utilized since 1974, when they were first revealed. The information is powerful and forms the necessary link between human and Divine, which creates the healing action. Humble yourself, drop all judgment, and allow yourself the gift of being open. Read, reread, and practice what you learn. Following these guidelines will bring you freedom, happiness, and immense rewards.

The Roadmap

Your Life Is Your Prayer

As You Live, So You Are

You Are The Maintainer and Creator Of Your Own Health And Reality

The More You Love And Bless Yourself And All Creation, The More Your Self And All Creation Loves And Blesses You

Live, Love, Enjoy And Appreciate The Gift Of Life

Love And Bless Yourself And All Creation Daily

And Be Filled With Life. Love and Light

Work At It, Achieve It, And Maintain It Through The Practice Of Living

Practice – Practice – Practice

All Day, Every Day

Give Thanks, Be Humble Always

And Remember

Life Begets Life

* * *

A Note From Erica: Following is the entire series of prayers by Howard Wills. If you have twenty minutes to do them all now, please do! If you are pressed for time, try to do at least the first one, the "Ancestral Prayer." As you pray, remember that the Divine does not forgive (because there is nothing to forgive!) and that this is an advanced way of thinking, being and living. Most of us need someplace to start; these prayers are that beginning place. Use them from a place of gentleness, softness and power, for yourself, your family and for all of humanity! Please stop, and do them now.

Ancestral Prayer

Lord, For Myself, My Spouse, All Our Family Members, All Our
Relationships, All Our Ancestors And All Their Relationships Back
Through All Time, Through All Of Our Lives

Lord, Please Help Us All Forgive, Be Forgiven, And All Forgive
Ourselves Completely And Totally, Now And Forever, Please Lord,
Thank You Lord (Repeat 3 Times)

Lord, Fill Us All With Your Love And Give Us All Complete Peace
Now And Forever, Please Lord, Thank You Lord (Repeat 3 Times)

Lord, We Thank You For Your Love, We Thank You For Your
Blessings, We Thank You For The Gift Of Life And All The Many Gifts
You Give Us Daily, Thank You Lord, Thank You Lord, Thank You Lord
(Repeat 3 Times)

Amen

Forgiveness Affirmation

I Bless This Day And Give Thanks For My Life

I Forgive Completely All People Who Have Hurt Me (Repeat 3 Times)

I Ask All People I Have Hurt To Please Forgive Me (Repeat 3 Times)

I Apologize To Myself For My Wrongs To Myself And My Wrongs To Others (Repeat 3 Times)

I Apologize For All My Hurts Or Wrongs To All Life Forms (Repeat 3 Times)

I Apologize For All My Hurts Or Wrongs To The Earth And The Life Of The Earth (Repeat 3 Times)

With This Release, Freedom, Peace, Power, And New Life, I Bless All Creation In The Entire Universe And I Fill The Entire Universe With My Love

I Love And Bless The Earth, All Life, And All Humanity

I Love, Bless, And Respect, The Visible, And The Invisible

I Rejoice And Give Thanks For My New Life, Power, And Health, And Give Complete Blessings And Love To All Life And All Creation Always

Prayer of Personal Forgiveness

I Bless This Day And Give Thanks For My Life

Lord In Heaven, I Am Your Child, Your Humble Child

I Give You My Love And Thank You For Your Constant Love And Blessings

Lord, I Ask That You Help Me Forgive And Release, Completely And Totally, All People Who Have Hurt Me Through Thought, Word Or Deed, Knowing Or Not Knowing

Please Lord, Please Lord, Thank You Lord, Thank You Lord, Thank You

Lord In Heaven, I Ask That You Help All People I Have Hurt Through Thought, Word Or Deed, Knowing Or Not Knowing, To Forgive And Release Me Completely And Totally

Please Lord, Please Lord, Thank You Lord, Thank You Lord, Thank You

Lord, I Ask That You Help Me Forgive And Release Myself Completely And Totally, For All The Times I Hurt Myself Or Hurt Others Through Thought, Word Or Deed, Knowing Or Not Knowing

Please Lord, Please Lord, Thank You Lord, Thank You Lord, Thank You

Lord In Heaven, I Ask That You Help All Life Forms I Have Hurt, In Any Way At Any Time To Forgive And Release Me Completely And Totally

Please Lord, Please Lord, Thank You Lord, Thank You Lord, Thank You

Lord In Heaven, I Ask That You Help Me To Be Forgiven And Released, Completely And Totally, For All My Hurts Or Wrongs To The

Earth And The Life Of The Earth Through Thought, Word Or Deed, Knowing Or Not Knowing

Please Lord, Please Lord, Thank You Lord, Thank You Lord, Thank You

With This Release, Freedom, Peace, Power, And New Life, I Bless All Creation In The Entire Universe And Fill The Entire Universe With My Love

I Love And Bless The Earth, All Life And All Humanity. I Love, Bless, And Respect, The Visible And The Invisible

I Rejoice And Give Thanks For My New Life, Power, And Health, And Give Complete Blessings And Love To All Life, Always

Thank You Lord In Heaven, Thank You Lord, Thank You

Prayer of Complete Personal Forgiveness

I Bless This Day And Give Thanks For My Life

Lord In Heaven, I Am Your Child, Your Humble Child

I Give You My Love, And I Thank You For Your Constant Love And Blessings

For All People Who Have Hurt Me – Mentally, Physically, Emotionally, Spiritually, Sexually, Financially, Or In Any Other Way Through Thought, Word Or Deed, Knowing Or Not Knowing

Lord In Heaven, I Ask That You Help Me Forgive And Release, Completely And Totally, All People Who Have Hurt Me

Please Lord, Please Lord, Thank You Lord, Thank You Lord, Thank You

And With God's Help, I Do Forgive And Release, Completely And Totally, All People Who Have Hurt Me

Thank You Lord In Heaven

For All People I Have Hurt – Mentally, Physically, Emotionally, Spiritually, Sexually, Financially, Or In Any Other Way Through Thought, Word Or Deed, Knowing Or Not Knowing

I Apologize To All Of You And Ask That You Please Forgive Me

Lord In Heaven, I Ask That You Help All People I Have Hurt Through Thought, Word Or Deed, Knowing Or Not Knowing, To Forgive And Release Me Completely And Totally

Please Lord, Please Lord, Thank You Lord, Thank You Lord, Thank You

And I Thank All People For Forgiving And Releasing Me Completely And Totally, With God's Help

Thank You Lord In Heaven
For All The Times I Hurt Myself – Mentally, Physically, Emotionally,
Spiritually, Sexually, Financially, Or In Any Other Way Through
Thought, Word Or Deed, Knowing Or Not Knowing

I Apologize To Myself For All My Hurts And Wrongs To Myself, And I
Ask To Be Forgiven

Lord In Heaven, I Ask That You Help Me Forgive And Release Myself
Completely And Totally
Please Lord, Please Lord, Thank You Lord, Thank You Lord, Thank
You

And With God's Help I Do Forgive And Release Myself Completely
And Totally

Thank You Lord In Heaven

For All Life Forms I Have Hurt In Any Way, At Any Time
I Apologize For My Hurts Or Wrongs To All Life Forms And I Ask To
Be Forgiven

Lord In Heaven, I Ask That You Help Me To Be Forgiven For My Hurts
Or Wrongs To All Life Forms

Please Lord, Please Lord, Thank You Lord, Thank You Lord, Thank
You

Thank You Lord For Helping Me To Be Forgiven For My Hurts Or
Wrongs To All Life Forms

Thank You Lord In Heaven

Lord In Heaven, I Ask That You Help Me To Be Forgiven For All My
Hurts Or Wrongs To The Earth And The Life Of The Earth Through
Thought, Word Or Deed, Knowing Or Not Knowing

Please Lord, Please Lord, Thank You Lord, Thank You Lord, Thank
You

Thank You Lord For Helping Me To Be Forgiven For All My Hurts Or
Wrongs To The Earth And The Life Of The Earth
Thank You Lord In Heaven

Lord, I Ask That You Bless All These Relationships, Fill Us With Your
Love, And Grant Us All Complete Peace, Now And Forever

Please Lord, Please Lord, Thank You Lord, Thank You Lord, Thank
You

Thank You Lord In Heaven

Prayer of Generational Forgiveness

Lord In Heaven, For Myself, All My Family Members, And All Our Ancestors, Back Through All Time, Through All Our Lives

For All People We Have Hurt, In Any Way At Any Time, We Apologize For All Our Hurts Or Wrongs And We Ask To Be Forgiven

Lord We Ask That You Help All People We Have Hurt, To Forgive And Release Us Completely And Totally, Now And Forever

Please Lord, Please Lord, Thank You Lord, Thank You Lord, Thank You Lord In Heaven

And We Thank All People For Forgiving And Releasing Us, Completely And Totally, With God's Help, Thank You Lord

Lord In Heaven, For Myself, All My Family Members, And All Our Ancestors, Back Through All Time, Through All Our Lives

Lord We Ask That You Help Us Forgive And Release, Completely And Totally, All People Who Have Hurt Us In Any Way, At Any Time

Please Lord, Please Lord, Thank You Lord, Thank You Lord, Thank You Lord In Heaven

And With God's Help, We Do Forgive And Release, Completely And Totally, All People Who Have Hurt Us, Thank You Lord

Lord In Heaven, For Myself, All My Family Members, And All Our Ancestors, Back Through All Time, Through All Our Lives

Lord, We Ask That You Help Us Forgive And Release Ourselves, Completely And Totally, For All The Times We Hurt Ourselves Or Hurt Others

Please Lord, Please Lord, Thank You Lord, Thank You Lord, Thank You Lord In Heaven

And With God's Help, We Do Forgive And Release Ourselves, Completely And Totally, For All The Times We Hurt Ourselves Or Hurt Others, Thank You Lord

Lord In Heaven, With This Release, Freedom, Peace, Power, And New Life, We Rejoice And Give Thanks For The Love, Life, Light, And Perfection We Are Now Receiving, Through Your Grace And Blessings

Now And Forever

Thank You Lord In Heaven, Thank You Lord, Thank You

Prayer for All Races, All Nations, All Humanity, The Earth, and All Life

Lord In Heaven, We Are Your Children, Your Humble Children

We Give You Our Love And We Thank You For Your Constant Love And Blessings

For All Races, All Nations, And All Humanity, Back Through All Time Through All Our Lives- For All Hurts And Wrongs We Have Done To Each Other, To Ourselves, To The Earth, And To The Life Of The Earth, Through Thought, Word Or Deed, Knowing Or Not Knowing, We Apologize For All Our Hurts And Wrongs And We Ask To Be Forgiven

Help Us Lord Please, To Forgive All Those Who Have Hurt Us, To Forgive Ourselves For The Times We Have Hurt Ourselves, And To Be Forgiven By All Those We Have Hurt

Please Lord, Please Lord, Thank You Lord, Thank You Lord, Thank You

And We Do Forgive And Release Each Other, Ourselves, And All Life, Completely And Totally, With God's Help, Thank You Lord

Lord In Heaven, Help Us Please To Have Reverence And Respect For All Life, And To Realize Our Responsibilities To Each Other, To Ourselves, To The Earth, And To All Life In The Creation Of Peace And Harmony For All Life During Our Lives

Help Us Lord, Please, To Attune Our Awareness, Our Intelligence, And Our Actions To The Inner Voice Of Goodness, Love, And Truth – You, Most High Lord In Heaven

Now And Forever

Thank You Lord In Heaven, Thank You Lord, Thank You

Prayer of Complete Healing for all Relationships

Lord In Heaven, We Are Your Children, Your Humble Children

We Give You Our Love And We Thank You For Your Constant Love And Blessings

We Ask Lord, Please, That You Lead Us, Guide Us, And Direct Us Into Your Life, Into Your Light, And Into Your Love

We Ask Lord, Please, That Your Perfection Become Our Perfection

That Your Love Become Our Love

That Your Life Become Our Life

And That Your Light Become Our Light

Mentally, Physically, Emotionally, Spiritually

And In All Ways Completely

We Thank You Lord For These Blessings

Thank You Lord For Your Love

We Ask Lord, Please, That You Join Us To Your Earth, To Your Heavens, To You, To All Creation, And To Ourselves – Minds To Feelings To Bodies In Peace, Life, Light, Love, And Perfection

We Ask Lord, Please, That Your Perfection Become Our Perfection

That Your Love Become Our Love

That Your Life Become Our Life

And That Your Light Become Our Light

Mentally, Physically, Emotionally, Spiritually

And In All Ways Completely

We Thank You Lord For This Freedom

Thank You Lord For Your Love

Thank You Lord For The Healing Of All These Relationships

Thank You Lord For The Gift Of Life

And All The Many Gifts You Give Us Always

Lord In Heaven, We Are Your Children, Your Humble Children

We Give You Our Love And We Thank You For Your Constant Love
And Blessings

We Bless All Your Creations In The Entire Universe

And We Fill The Entire Universe With Our Love

We Bless The Earth, The Moon, The Planets, The Sun All Stars, And All
Celestial Bodies

We Bless The Trees, The Plants, The Flowers, The Waters, The Fish,
The Birds, The Wind, The Insects, The Animals, All Humanity, And All
Life On Earth, And In The Entire Universe

And We Fill All Things, All Time, All Space, And All Dimensions With
Our Love As We Celebrate This Gift Of Freedom, Life, Love, And
Healing

Now And Forever

Thank You Lord In Heaven, Thank You Lord, Thank You

Prayer of Complete Personal Healing

Lord In Heaven, I Am Your Child, Your Humble Child

I Give You My Love And I Thank You For Your Constant Love And Blessings

I Ask Lord, Please, That You Lead Me, Guide Me, And Direct Me Into Your Life, Into Your Light, And Into Your Love

I Ask Lord, Please, That Your Perfection Become My Perfection

That Your Love Become My Love

That Your Life Become My Life

And That Your Light Become My Light

Mentally, Physically, Emotionally, Spiritually

And In All Ways Completely

I Thank You Lord For These Blessings

Thank You Lord For Your Love

I Ask Lord, Please, That You Join Me To Your Earth, To Your Heavens, To You, To All Creation, And To Myself, Mind To Feelings To Body In Peace, Life, Light, Love, And Perfection

I Ask Lord Please That Your Perfection Become My Perfection

That Your Love Become My Love

That Your Life Become My Life

And That Your Light Become My Light

Mentally, Physically, Emotionally, Spiritually
And In All Ways Completely

I Thank You Lord For This Freedom

Thank You Lord For Your Love

Thank You Lord For My Healing

Thank You Lord For The Gift Of Life

And All The Many Gifts You Give Me Always

Lord In Heaven, I Am Your Child, Your Humble Child

I Give You My Love And I Thank You For Your Constant Love And Blessings

I Bless All Your Creations In The Entire Universe

And I Fill The Entire Universe With My Love

I Bless The Earth, The Moon, The Planets, The Sun

All Stars And All Celestial Bodies

I Bless The Trees, The Plants, The Flowers, The Waters, The Fish, The Birds, The Wind, The Insects, The Animals, All Humanity, And All Life On Earth, And In The Entire Universe

And I Fill All Things, All Time, All Space, And All Dimensions With My Love, As I Celebrate This Gift Of Freedom, Life, Love, And Healing

Now And Forever

Thank You Lord In Heaven, Thank You Lord, Thank You

Prayer of Thanks

I Have Made Peace And Have Opened My Entire Being To The Light And Power Of Life And God

I Join Myself With This Seen And Unseen Presence In Respect And Humility

I Have Reverence For All That Is

With This New Station And Position In Life, I Reach Outward And Reach Inward To Claim For Myself A Perfect, Happy, Healthy, Body, Mind, And Spirit, Free Of All Past Problems Or Illnesses

And As I Live My Life, I Am Living With Complete Perfect Natural Health

I Live Free, I Live Healthy, I Live

Thank You Lord In Heaven, Thank You Lord

Thank You Lord, Thank You Lord

Now And Forever

Thank You Lord

Amen

The Prayer of Bounty

Lord, Please Open My Mind, Heart, And Being To Your Complete Limitless, Bountiful Prosperity, And Love

Please Help All Things That I Think, Say, And Do Be Filled With Your Complete Limitless, Bountiful Prosperity And Love

Please Allow Me To Be Blessed With The Riches And Bounty Of Your Heavens And Your Earth Always

Please Lead Me, Guide Me, And Direct Me Into Your Life, Into Your Light, Into Your Love, And Into Your Complete Limitless, Bountiful Prosperity, And Love Celebrating Life As The Gift It Is From You Lord, Now And Forever

Thank You Lord, Thank You Lord, Thank You Lord, Thank You Lord, Thank You Lord, Thank You Lord, Thank You Lord, Thank You Amen

The Prayer of Freedom

Lord In Heaven,
For Me, My Family And All Humanity
Throughout All Time
Please Help Us Forgive All People
Help All People Forgive Us
And Help Us All Forgive Ourselves
Please Lord, Thank you Lord, Amen
Help Us All Love Each Other And Love
Ourselves
Be At Peace With Each Other And Be
At Peace With Ourselves
Please Lord, Thank Lord Amen
Lord, We Give You Our Love
And Thank You For Your Constant
Love And Blessings
We Bless All Your Creations
And We Fill All Your Creations With
Our Love
Lord, We Give You Our Love
And Thank You For Your Constant
Love And Blessings
We Bless All Your Creations
And We Fill All Your Creations With
Our Love
Lord, Please Open, Bless, Empower,
Expand
Lead, Guide, Direct And Protect
Me, My Family And All Humanity
Throughout All Time
Now And Forever
Please Lord, Thank You Lord
Amen, Amen, Amen, Amen

The Forgiveness List:
An Exercise in Freeing Yourself.

Take out a piece of paper and make a list of all of the people you are upset with, or who may be upset with you. I usually include myself on this list, *as all forgiveness is self forgiveness.* Include people who have passed on, as well. No one is going to see this so please be brutally honest with yourself.

Once your list is complete, ask the Divine to make you aware of anyone else you may be holding any negativity or resentment against, in even the slightest way. Set a strong intention to turn everything over to the Divine, and ask the Presence to take all of this heaviness from you and free you. You may even decide to prostrate and lay the list and all it represents at the feet of the Divine.

When you are ready, place the forgiveness list on your lap and put your hands gently on top of it. While you have your hands on the paper, gaze and contemplate the following picture that has been infused with Divine Grace.

As you receive this Grace Blessing, ask the Divine Presence to help you in setting your relationships right, or to guide you in how to make them right. Relax and allow it to happen. Please gaze at the art for a few minutes, then close your eyes and rest for twenty minutes or longer.

Once you open your eyes, take at least one long slow deep breath, and release. Get up and walk around the room; take notice of how you feel in your mind, body and emotions. Sit down and look at the list of people. What do you notice? Has anything changed?

Many people find that they feel lighter after this exercise. When they look at the list of names again, they feel neutral about most or even all of them. They are finally free, and they didn't have to "work" on a single thing! Grace lifted the burdens, pain and resentments right up and out of them!

If you still do not feel neutral about everyone on the list, that is alright, too. Let it go for now; see how you feel in a week or so. When serious hurts and traumas have occurred, there can be a lot of unwanted emotion tied up in the event. For these situations, do the *Mastery of Mind and Emotion* process found elsewhere in this book. Fully and completely feel into all of the feelings you have. Drop any stories around the situation and just feel the emotions. Your power and freedom lies in purely feeling!

Remember that you are the only one judging the situation. The Divine does not judge, ever. Get your power back, and free yourself through forgiveness!

Additional Resource:
The "Flying on the Wings of Love" program was inspired by Howard Wills prayers; it can be found at: http://shop.ericarock.com/flying-on-the-wings-of-love/ The program's prayers include forgiveness and peacemaking then go beyond, bringing you into a state of Love Consciousness. There is a simplified and quicker version of the prayers and an additional peacemaking exercise included to set you free from any and all resentment. It culminates with a Grace Blessing at the end to assist you in gaining the freedom you so desire!

Create a God that Works for You

Going within for the answers you seek is easier if you have a form of the Divine that resonates with you.

Notice that the Presence will make itself known as Jesus to Christians and Catholics, manifest as Lord Shiva or Ganesha to Indians, and appear simply as formless light to someone into Metaphysics. It seems that the Divine shows itself as what you believe Him/Her to be, whatever form is best for *you* to relate to. That is how important you are to the Divine; the Presence is delighted to make itself known to you in any manner that you choose!

In Truth, there is only One being in the entire Universe. Each and every one of us is a focal point of the ONE, so it is important that you find a personal relationship with God that works for you. The Presence loves you, supports you and wishes you to have everything that you desire for yourself. It wants to connect to you in ways that you can accept!

So cultivate the image of a Divine form that feels good and right to you, one that you can relate and speak to comfortably. Imagine in God all of the qualities that you would want in the ultimate parent and caregiver: like humor, gentleness, cherishing, support, caring, love. Whatever you feel you needed and didn't receive as a child, use that to help create the image of God you will work with. There are infinite possibilities, so ask for whatever you desire! Make it fun and exciting.

The Presence will behave the way you expect, and the results in your life will reflect those expectations as well.

Create a God with this in mind and you will see how amazing, easy and graceful your life will become! God will become a reality for you rather than a mind construct, and the Presence will be at your beck and call for any and all of your life's issues, down to the most mundane. The Presence cares about each and every aspect of our day to day lives. Nothing is too small or inconsequential, nothing is too big or grand - it is only our human minds that put the limitations on what the Source cares about and can accomplish. The Source has no limits!

The assistance of Grace from this book will deepen your relationship with the Creator even more, so create this personal image of God with confidence.

* * *

Building a Divine Relationship

After years of feeling separate from God, the Presence finally feels like an inner long lost friend to me. God listens to me, communicates with me and co-creates my glorious life with me. I feel safe, protected, loved, powerful, supported, cherished and looked after in all areas of my life. God handles each and every detail for me, as long as I remember to ask.

You can speak with God in any way that feels comfortable to you; God is not hung up on formalities. Sometimes we can get stuck on our ideas of how to address God; the mind gets in the way. The Presence doesn't care about this, it simply wants to have a relationship with you. I find that speaking with the Presence just as I would anyone else that I am close with works quite well.

Now I'd like you to stop reading for a moment, and close your eyes. Go within and tell the Presence that you would like to reformulate your relationship with Him/Her. Ask that it be filled with all of the attributes that you want from your God. Let the Divine create a new, life supportive relationship with you that will last for eternity.

Whatever you want in life, simply ask for it, let go and receive. Every prayer is heard and answered - *every prayer, every request.* You only have to let go and get out of the way! All of your doubt, worry, judgment, criticism, scorn, pride, and worries about what you have or don't have? Those things just get in the way of receiving your hearts desires. You have to learn to *let it go.*

Let go of the belief that you have to "earn" things in life. Let go of thinking that life is about learning lessons and paying karma. You can choose to believe those things if you want, but does that belief seem life-supportive and empowering? Life does not have to be about learning lessons or earning rewards. Grace supersedes all of that, if you let it.

Create a relationship with the Creator that is such that you are showered with everything that you could ever want, need or desire, so that it comes to you with ease and grace. The Grace Blessings will help you with this. You will soon find yourself in a place where you can simply think of something, without making a formal prayer or request, and it will come to you!

* * *

Deepening the Relationship Within

Take time out daily to be still and converse with God, to ask for help and guidance when you need it. The response may come in various forms: a voice, a feeling, a thought, a knowing, a vision. Answers may come through other people or outside events. You need to become acutely aware, notice, feel, observe; learn to listen for the answers, however they show up.

Speak with the Divine like a dear friend and confidant; this gives you a chance to receive the guidance and nurturing that your soul so yearns for. This can be the ultimate homecoming so many of us have longed for! Take time throughout that day to give thanks to the Divine for all of the wonderful blessings that have shown up in your life as well. We tend to only speak to God when the going gets rough, which is perfectly fine. But how wonderful it is to stop, go within and give thanks when things are going well.

The silent retreat I offer is a chance to take everything to the Presence, bringing all thoughts, feelings, memories and any questions you may have to the Source within. The deeper into the silence you go, the deeper the relationship with the Divine. Your relationship with the Divine grows until it becomes such a precious priority that you won't want to speak!

Your inner light ignites, the flame burning luminous. That spark will remain lit always, unless you choose otherwise. You are finally awake, aware and connected. You feel stronger, unsinkable, able to respond to circumstances with great care and love, no longer reacting from past programming. When you take all thoughts, feelings and experiences to the Presence within, you become free and liberated.

So give everything over at the feet of the Divine! Take all of your old, sad stories and hurt feelings, and surrender them within! Old hurts, burdens, pain, strife and struggle can dissipate into nothingness. Reclaim your power from external authorities. Stop seeking answers, guidance, nurturing and comfort from the outside; take it all *within,* and you will reclaim vast amounts of power! You can be free forever.

The Divine is willing to answer any need or question you have. As you open to this, you will begin to receive inspirations from within; solutions appear from out of nowhere. So vow to yourself, now, to take everything within as much as possible. Before you pick up the phone and call your psychic, your friend, your mother, father, counselor or anyone else, take your concern to the Presence. Sit, close your eyes, go within, look inside yourself. Everything you ever need is right there!

Soon, you will be so firmly led from within that you will have little need for outside help. Your awakening is already underway, and it will be deepened by practicing silence. Try taking hours or days at a time to be silent, to listen to that still soft voice within you. The rewards are grand!

If you have been resisting feeling for the majority of your life, sitting in silence can be difficult, but it gets easier with practice. As you dare to feel and nurture the most important relationship in the world, the relationship with yourself and the Presence, the silence becomes sweet and rejuvenating.

The evening I wrote this, I was literally buzzing with loving energy. I lay down on my bed, intentionally inviting more life force into my being through breath, and I was transported into a blissful ecstatic state. I felt every molecule of my being as love. The deeper I dove into the feeling, the stronger and more intense it became. I dove fully into it! The loving feeling expanded, growing within and around me; it was as though the entire universe was inside of my heart.

I look forward to taking time out each day this way, to just be with myself, to sit, breathe and feel. The more I do this, the more magical and enchanting life becomes for me. I did have to fully experience plenty of lower vibrational emotions before reaching this place in my journey. I approached my feelings eagerly, ready to feel them completely. I let go of my fear of them, and gave myself the gift of mastering the mind and emotions.

This does not mean that I don't get frustrated or angry. Oh no, not at all. I still experience ALL emotions. I just don't judge myself for them and I practice not judging my life experiences. Keep in mind it has taken me awhile to get here, by practicing everything I have laid out for you in these pages.

Being human, we *are* a feeling. We feel emotions in each and every moment. It is the natural state of being human; we cannot escape emotion. So give yourself the gift of freedom and love, and accept your feelings in every moment of every day.

The Grace Blessings that you are receiving from the artwork within this book will help you to tap into the unlimited powerful resources within, to find strength in silence, to accept your feelings. Welcome them!

* * *

The Mind Likes to Question

When you take everything to the Presence within, you'll find that questions you've had for a lifetime are answered simply. Other questions will simply dissolve and lose any meaning or relevance. Most of our questions are just our mind doing what it loves to do: analyze, figure out, categorize, name and label. It's what the mind does! As you receive Grace Blessings, the mind chatter begins to subside. In that silence, the voice of the Infinite can be heard through your heart; a certain *knowing* within you emerges.

As humans, we ask "why" a lot, but there is no "why" in life. Life is simply for living! All of these distractions of the mind keep us from living to our fullest potential. Stop asking why and go out and live your life! That is what you came here to do, nothing more and nothing less; *you came here to live.*

The Creator plants seeds within each of us, natural gifts and talents available for us to develop. Cultivating those seeds brings us sheer joy; it's the greatest gift that we can give back to the Source! Whatever brings you joy, whatever you are naturally talented at, those are the things you came here to do. Whether you are paid for it or not is irrelevant. These gifts are what you are here for.

As your mind becomes more peaceful, you'll truly begin to live in the now. You'll start to ask different sorts of questions, things like "What would I like to do today?" "What would feel good to do in this moment?" "What would I enjoy creating next?" and so on.

If your mind becomes cluttered or you feel confused, just lay the clutter down at the feet of the Divine. Take a breath, and peace will be restored to you, putting you back in the present, the moment of now. Those feelings of confusion, frustration or irritation are there to let you know to slow down. When you feel them, take a break, recalibrate yourself. By sitting quietly and allowing the space in our minds to clear, we can discern the answers we seek. In silence, a new consciousness opens up for us. With the new consciousness, problems get resolved. Problems and struggles can only function in the consciousness that created them; shift consciousness and shift your life.

* * *

Another Question of the Mind

I'm often asked "How do I know when I am receiving true Divine guidance?"

In every moment, we are receiving messages from the Divine. To hear the guidance, you must become quiet and still. The voice of the Infinite is not usually a burning bush experience, but a soft voice. It may sound like your own voice, but very wise. When you hear it, it will open your heart and make you feel really good inside.

How Can It Get Any Better Than This?

Our mind likes to question, and sometimes, it tells scary what-if stories - dramatic stories that trigger unwanted emotion and send us on a roller coaster in our heads. How dreadful to be terrified of something that might happen! Most of the time, that "what-if" never manifests; what a waste of bliss space and energy, all because of the mind's questions!

Let's play with questions for a moment, so you can learn more about the mind.

What happens if I ask you *"How would you feel right now having a piece of cheesecake"?* Where did your mind go? Your mind is busy eating cheesecake now, isn't it?

I have found it useful to have a question handy for the mind to chase after, a question that keeps it busy. It should be a question that always works, feels good no matter what is going on around us, a question that is empowering.

The one I use is "How can it get any better than this?" If I get out of bed and stub my toe, I ask "How can it get any better than this?" If I have a wonderful day and feel absolutely marvelous I ask, "How can it get any better than this?" If someone gives me $500.00, I say "How can it get any better than this?" I find myself stuck in traffic on the way to an appointment, I ask, "How can it get any better than this?"

This single question always cheers me up instantly. It raises my vibration and gets me in the flow of life once again. If I am already high, it propels me even higher. It is effective and appropriate at all times, and during all circumstances.

So if you find your mind wanting to ask scary questions, give it something useful to chase after. Ask empowering questions!

Try these:

How might I feel when ....?
What is my life going to look like when........?
What are some of the possibilities here?

What is the highest and best outcome for all involved?
How might I see this from a more empowering perspective?
How can it get any better than this?
Wouldn't it be nice if...........?
Isn't it going to be fun when...........?

***Additional Resource:** Please share your questions and results with me on my members forum at my website, http://www.ericarock.com We have built a wonderful, supportive and fun community where we share our triumphs, victories, and celebrations. We find a lot of assistance, guidance and support from each other there, and you're welcome to join us!*

You Can Shift Reality in the Blink of an Eye

As you open to Grace Blessings, you will find that the Universe can and will tilt for you! The mind cannot understand how this works; it is not a concept, it is an experience. Through this experience, you will discover that there are no rules to life or reality. We get to make up the rules as we go along! The only limits are the ones in our own minds.

Part of the game we play here on Earth is agreeing to rules and limitations. We agree to gravity. We agree that matter is dense and solid, that disease is a part of life, that we age and have to die. These rules shape our experience of reality, but *they are all illusions.* We can change the rules of the game at anytime. You will be able to do this soon, I promise!

Some of us enjoy rules more than others. The more heavily invested we are in the "rules" of our life, the more hesitant we feel about letting go of the perceived limitations. But when we open to the unlimited possibilities available to us, and forget about the rules, we can have, do or be anything that we desire.

Stop for a moment and let that soak in: *You can have, do or be whatever you desire!*

When you read that sentence, you may hear negative thoughts or experience unwanted feelings. That is perfectly alright. Those feelings are just information. They are letting you know that you have contradictory beliefs about the statement, that you don't quite believe it is true. You may not have enough evidence that this is true yet. That is OK, you will soon!

I've participated in many fire walk ceremonies, and they amaze me every time. In the group dynamic, we all decide that we are going to be able to walk on fire and not get burned. Guess what? No one is burned! We *disrespect reality* and we break the rule that says that hot coals will burn you.

As our consciousness expands, we delight in breaking the rules. We begin to think, "Well, if I can do *that,* what else can I do?" Life starts to get really magical and exciting. Grace Blessings even override the Law of Attraction, because the Grace gives us an energetic boost in the direction of our heart's desires.

Have you ever noticed that when something incredible happens, the mind wants to automatically dismiss it, to erase it as though it didn't happen? Some things are just too big, grand and immense for the mind to wrap around, so it dismisses them. These big things are against the rules!

Stop for a moment, and think about how your need for rules may be holding you back. Think about your beliefs about yourself, the limitations you put on other people. Those limits and beliefs are a prison of your own creation.

What could happen if you said, "Yes, I am open to life and to all possibilities?" Consider what your life would look like if there were no rules at all. With some openness, reality could shift for you at a moment's notice!

Take a moment to breathe in that idea; notice how that makes you feel inside.

A Real Life Example

My dear friend Andy is a great example of how breaking the rules works; he had an unconscious belief that it is not OK to receive. This worldview made it difficult for Grace to deliver all of the love, abundance and blessings that were trying to come through for him. He couldn't receive it, because it was against the "rules"!

He felt conflicted, unwanted feelings because of his belief, so he used the Mastery of Mind and Emotions practice to fully feel into the feelings. As he felt into them, he had the realization that he didn't feel comfortable receiving. As he felt into the next set of feelings, he was able to come to a truer and thus more empowering realization:
"Our Creator wants to give us absolutely everything. Our gift back to God is to receive, receive, receive!"

Andy had already felt the truth of this deep in his heart, but he had to feel into the feelings first, so he could come to this new place of expanded consciousness. Nothing is holding him back now in his new, more empowering and truthful worldview! He is in a very powerful place, creating miracle after miracle in his life. The tension and conflict he had felt are gone. He is creating and expanding his consciousness more and more each day. Doors and opportunities are flying open for him. He keeps me abreast on the current "miracles" in his life, and I delight in his victories!

We are teaching your mind to let go, to stop believing in the rules, just like Andy.

Separated From God

Do sometimes you feel out of place, as though you've been dropped off on the wrong planet and are waiting for your spaceship to pick you up?

When we feel separate from God, we often do not want to be here. I've felt like that. I remember being a teenager, bounding out of my bedroom one afternoon and exclaiming to my mother, "I wish I was stupid! I know too much and it hurts and I want out of here!" My mom nearly keeled over at that remark; she did not know what to say to comfort me. I was angry as hell at the morons who dreamed up this entire human experiment, and I wanted to fire them!

The problem was that I felt separated from Source. Most people do.

Of course, we *are* Source, in human form! How in the heck can we possibly be disconnected from that which we are? We can't - it is a false paradox. The feelings of separation are an illusion, a misperception of the Truth.

The Grace Blessings you're receiving will assist you in knowing the Truth of yourself, that you are connected, you do belong. Any feeling of separation will dissolve. You will gradually move from having a relationship with the Divine, to knowing you *are* the Divine.

I am on this journey with you - I am not totally to that place of full knowing, yet, myself. But I have glimpses of this experience, of really knowing *I AM* the Divine in physical form. Grace will help us to have this awareness, to have a fully awake body and a flowered heart. Being able to give and receive love freely is our birthright; nothing feels better than love; love really is all we need.

Many people carry a lot of pain in their body and heart, and of course they want off of this planet! But if we learn to flow all emotion, to lay down all of our heaviness and hurt at the feet of the Divine, we won't want to leave anymore. As you progress, you will enjoy being human and on this planet. I thoroughly *love* my humanness.

That was not always true for me, and I know it isn't true for many others. But it will be true for you! This *is* the place to be, you are always in the right place at the right time. Feel the truth of that statement, and you can let go of all limitations and "mistakes", knowing there is no wrong place, and no mistakes, ever.

From Drama to Ease

Once your awakening has begun, your life becomes more drama free. At first, this new life may feel a little flat. As drama gives way to ease, flow and connection, things may feel a little odd and unfamiliar. You may even think you miss the drama. But you can get all the drama you want through books and movies; you do not need to create grand painful dramas in your life! Feed the drama-loving part of you in a healthy way, and you'll have no need to create unhealthy manifestations.

If you're used to a life full of seeking and healing and therapy, when you find God and open to Grace, you'll have so much more free time and energy! At first, you may not know how to fill the space in your life that used to be consumed with constantly clearing, fixing and working on "issues".

Live your life! Do whatever you enjoy! Take a class for fun, get a hobby, get three hobbies. You will have more time to create, make love, laugh, exercise, paint, draw, dance and sing. Life will flow more easily for you, more of the time. Inspirations, solutions, people, events and circumstances will show up already designed as a winning situation for everyone.

Your only job is to let go, feel good, relax and allow the invisible force that unifies all to align you with what you need and desire. Do not stress or worry about when your full Enlightenment will come. The process has begun; there is nothing else for you to do.

Your Enlightenment will happen in Divine Time.

Meditating

People often ask me what spiritual practices I use, and if I meditate.

I answer them honestly, saying "Daily, I do what I am guided and lead to do. I do what makes me feel good." But I do like to meditate and go within. I am not trying to achieve anything while I meditate; I am doing it for the pure joy of feeling my physical body and to consciously breathe and rejoice in being alive.

When you meditate, do what feels good for you. Just sit, get quiet, breathe and observe. Go into it with a playfulness, asking, "Let's see what happens when I do this…" Let go of any goals of attaining a certain spiritual state, outcome, or result. Go into meditation and into life in general with an attitude of openness and curiosity.

A Practice of Appreciation

Appreciation for all that you have opens you to more Blessings. The most powerful prayer you can ever make is "Thank you!"

Train yourself to tell the Source "thank you" for everything; shower appreciation on all that is good in your life. Use your free will to intentionally focus on the positives, to really *appreciate* them. Some people have trouble expressing gratitude, but everyone can find something to appreciate. Cultivating this simple habit makes such a difference in our lives!

If you practice appreciation first thing in the morning, it sets a positive tone for the whole day. Upon awakening, lie in your bed and let your mind run through all that is going well in your life, then continue to take time throughout your day to appreciate all that you have. Choosing to show appreciation is a powerful and positive use of the gift of free will.

Focusing on the good in life will raise your vibration, expanding your consciousness so there is room to allow even more good in. Feelings of appreciation release hormones and chemicals in the brain, helping us to feel good and healthy. Appreciation deepens the breath response, affects our respiration, improves digestion and increases blood flow; focusing on what feels good is actually medicine for the body! Appreciation also helps to bring us strongly in alignment with our Divine self, because our Divine self never focuses on anything unwanted.

Whatever it is that you desire, you will receive it in Divine time. Maybe it's a new love, enlightenment, new career, or new home that you want to have. If you can relax, let go and be open to receive, it will show up! Look around you, notice and appreciate any part of what you want that you *already have*, and the rest of it will come to you more quickly. If you would like a new relationship, focus on the areas of your life where you are already letting love in, in all of its glorious forms. When you are out in the world, take notice of all of the happy loving couples that you come across. Their love is your love! Want more abundance in your life? Place your focus on all of the prosperity you already have, and more will come to you.

If you want a new job, focus on the good parts of your current job. Be appreciative of the people you work with. Maybe the drive to work is pleasant - you can enjoy and focus on that. Look for the aspects of what you desire that are already in your life, the things that already bring you happiness. Appreciate them to the maximum!

When we begin a relationship, start a job, or move into a home, there are exciting things to enjoy and appreciate. After a while, we take those things for granted. We turn our focus on the unwanted aspects, and things start to go south. When we focus on what we don't like and don't want, we attract more that is unwanted. When we appreciate the things we do want, we attract the positives into our life.

So if you're struggling with a situation that has turned sour, sit and reminisce about whatever you originally enjoyed about it. This will shift your vibration back to appreciation, and you'll get to a place where things feel better. When you start to feel better about the situation, you know you are on the right track!

Developing a practice of appreciation will raise your vibration while you are waiting for your desires to manifest. If lower emotional vibrations creep back up, embrace them, say "yes" to those feelings. They will move up in altitude and shift things for you.

If you are having difficulty with feeling appreciation, or find that you're still focused on what isn't in your life, fully feel into those feelings using the exercises found elsewhere in this book. The full "Mastery of Mind and Emotions" program that I've mentioned elsewhere can also to help you fully allow and experience the recurrent low vibrational feelings around "not having it yet."

Physical Illness

As you receive Grace Blessings, a lot of lower vibrational energy may start to move within you. When you set the intention to put down a lifetime of baggage and let go of past hurts, you may feel as if you're in a storm of energy and emotion. It will pass quickly, if you do not resist it. Let go and allow the energy to move. If you feel it, it is moving; that is good news! Some people will feel the changes emotionally, others will feel them physically – your experience will depend on how comfortable you are with feeling emotions. *A physical symptom is nothing more than an energetic vibration.*

Doctors put scary labels on things; they show us evidence of problems, and maybe we see direct evidence of dis-ease in our bodies. It can be difficult to relax in the face of all this! So hold the desired image of health in your mind with unwavering confidence. Stay open to the possibility of the Divine healing you, and do what you feel guided to do.

Know this Truth: *We create reality by observing it.*

When we observe *"what is"*, we vibrate in alignment with *what is*, and reality brings us more of *what is*.

Anything that physically manifests, good or bad, is due to you vibrating in tune with it for a period of time. So if you notice even the slightest improvement in your condition, put a *HUGE* amount of focus, attention and appreciation on that improvement. Vibrate on the level of that positive *"what is."* Rave to the nines about the improvement! Get on the phone and tell everyone you know about it. You can speak that new reality of health into existence.

We often receive what we speak about. If you are sick or ill in any way, I encourage you *not* to tell everyone. Talking about it gets you into the story around the illness, and encourages you to move into a "woe is me" attitude. That only creates more woe, more drama, more feeling ill! Instead, focus on the positive. Speak the wellness into "what is"!

I know being diagnosed with a physical disease can be scary. Remember that the symptoms are just a vibration of energy. The physical manifestation is trying to tell you something, so pay attention. It's important information. At the bottom of every physical issue is a *feeling* that has not been fully felt or experienced.

Ask "What feeling is underneath this?" The answer will help you know more about how to heal yourself.

The energy contained within this artwork is specifically tuned for assisting with physical healing. Please gaze at the artwork for a few minutes, then close your eyes and rest for twenty or more minutes. When you get up, walk around the room and take careful notice of how your body feels. Note the subtle or not so subtle changes. Rave to the mountaintops about any improvements. You are returning to your perfection!

Additional Resource: If you are dealing with any illness or pain and you are not seeing better results through the use of this book, there are deeper resources through private sessions. You'll find more information at the end of this book.

The Importance of Conscious Breathing

We are alive because we breathe. Becoming aware of your breath is a powerful practice. It will take you deeper into your consciousness, and can free you from the pains and burdens you carry. Deep breathing helps us be fully present in our bodies, and being fully present allows us to *fully feel.* Conscious breathing is excellent for dealing with stress whenever it occurs; the techniques are so simple they can be done anywhere, anytime. Breathing keeps us connected to ourselves and to life; it moves energy, and as our energy moves our lives can move in new, interesting and positive ways. Breathing is liberating!

The breath *is* Spirit, and we can invite the Divine into our body through our breath. Breathe consciously and deliberately, *now.* Take long slow deep breaths, filling your body with the breath of life, of light!

Tragically, most people are barely breathing enough to be alive. Breathing is a key to a healthy body; cancer, pathogens and viruses cannot live in oxygen. Breathing is also key for a healthy attitude - it is physiologically impossible to be angry and breathe simultaneously.

Try it sometime! When you find yourself feeling down or plagued by other lower vibrational emotions, do 5-20 minutes of deep breathing. You will feel different afterward. When you sit with yourself, when you get still and breathe, it opens you to the voice and guidance of the Infinite.

Circular Breathing

One method I'd like you to learn is called circular breathing. Take a long deep breath in through your mouth, then release it again, like a long sigh. There is no pause between the inhalations and exhalations; you will be breathing in a continuous circle. It will feel quite intense, and may even make you feel dizzy. Most deep breathing exercises will make you feel dizzy until you are used to them; it is a lot of oxygen flooding you at once.

As you breathe this way, you may also experience physical sensations in your body, or emotions may well up. Celebrate it! The sensations are energy moving; these energies need to move or they fester and cause disease. If you feel them, it is because they are moving on and moving out, so feeling them is a good sign. If you are feeling, if you are breathing, you are alive!

This simple practice of circular breathing reduces stress, opens you to the Divine, and sets the stage for healing on all levels. Practicing it regularly brings great benefit.

* * *

About Other Methods

Another of my favorite breathing meditations is the Ananda Mandala. It is a chakra clearing and breathing meditation that awakens the kundalini, clears and opens all of the energy centers. Guided recordings of the full practice are available through Amazon, Napster and iTunes. I highly recommend it!

The Ananda Mandala has been called the circle of bliss; during it, people often break into hysterical laughter for no apparent reason! This way of breathing moves a lot of old energy and emotion. It is only about 20-25 minutes in length, so it's easy to do. It's best if you practice it on a regular basis; making it a habit first thing in the morning, at sunrise or at sunset is perfect. For maximum benefit, try this in a group while holding hands.

There are many other breathing methods and techniques out there to try; find a pattern of breathing that works for *you*. Conscious breathing is simple and healthy. It will invigorate and rejuvenate you. As you explore your breath, it is *so* important to listen to your body, what it needs, what it enjoys. Follow your own way!

I've given a few methods and suggestions for conscious breathing here, but if they don't fit for you, that is fine. To discover what worked for me, I simply lay in bed one night and experimented. I found the patterns that fit my breath, and did that. Simple enough!

Explore, have fun with this. Honor yourself, love your body, treat it well. Feed it oxygen, the greatest food for the body. It is abundantly available!

Conscious breathing has been a primary practice for me throughout my unfolding and awakening process. I speak about it because it is effective, and I know you will feel and see immediate results in your life.

Extra Suggestion: *Try taking breathing exercises into the workplace, schools, hospitals, or hospice centers. See what kinds of magic happens.*

Your Mind Is Trying to Help You

In the past, when I would have a negative thought or painful memory, I would freeze, tense up and go into fear. It felt like an attack. The fear would produce anger, and I felt in conflict with myself, my mind and my emotions.

Now, when I have a painful memory, I know that this is only my mind attempting to show me where I need to forgive myself, forgive someone else, or shift a limiting belief. It's trying to tell me how I can be free!

The other day, a memory of hurtful things an old roommate once said to me rose up. Instead of feeling like I was under attack (which is a victim vibration) I welcomed the memory and realized that this was my mind trying to show me where I was holding resentment and pain in my own body. It was showing me where I needed to forgive.

I don't want to be holding any pain or resentment toward anyone, so I thanked the thought for trying to help me, then took the opportunity I was being given. I dove deeply into the emotion so that I could fully experience it. By the time I finished, I was feeling complete compassion toward myself and my former roommate. I even began to laugh at the entire event - it now felt and seemed quite funny to me.

* * *

A client recently gave another example of this in action:

She awoke on the morning of our scheduled session with painful memories of old relationships. She needed to do some forgiving, that much she knew. But during the session she had a deeper realization that the person she needed to forgive was *herself!*

Because she'd already been receiving Grace Blessings, and energy was moving within her, she'd had many memories bubble up to the surface of her consciousness. They were showing her instances where she had hurt other people. These memories had really upset her; she was feeling unworthy, guilty and bad for her past behaviors and actions.

In our session, I explained that the memories were simply trying to show her where she needed to forgive herself. Once she realized that her mind was producing these memories to try to *help* her, she saw that they were a gift. She began to welcome and embrace them. We spoke about taking all of the hurt and prostrating, giving it over to the Presence.

She is feeling very worthy these days. She's soft and gentle with herself as well as other people, and she feels light, happy and full of energy. Before these sessions, she had referred to herself as a low energy person. Well of course! She was carrying all of that shame around; it had really weighed her down. She has let it all go now. You can, too.

* * *

My Own Unfolding

During my own unfolding process, I had two straight weeks of awful memories, horrible thoughts centered around my family and things that occurred during childhood. I made things worse for myself by judging how I was feeling about it, refusing the emotions, and resisting feeling altogether.

I had a habit of running from things like this, of stuffing them down and distracting myself. But these scenes in my mind were persistent! Finally, I had enough of them; I got angry! I took it to the Presence. I sat with the feelings and asked, "What is the gift here for me?"

I quickly saw that there was much from my childhood and past that I was hanging onto and not forgiving, including myself. Those buried feelings were creating in my reality, continuing some familial patterns that were not serving anyone.

So I asked the Divine for help. I prostrated. I allowed myself to *fully experience and feel all of my feelings* as they arose. Soon, I was free and feeling lighter. An entire life's worth of family stuff quickly moved on through me. I felt it shift as it came into my consciousness, and left again.

I didn't expect my family members to change, I just went within myself, gave it over to the Presence. I surrendered, and at last I could finally hear the Divine speaking, telling me, "This is an opportunity for more openness, love and healing for you and your entire family, if you choose to see it that way."

Thankfully I made that choice, and I had beautiful heartfelt talks with my sister, mother and step father. I came to them from a neutral place that was full of love. My goal was to elicit openness and understanding, so I was very deliberate in how I communicated with them. We have open, relaxed, real talks now. There is more love and compassion among all of us than ever before. I can say that I truly love them all unconditionally, *exactly as they are.*

The two weeks of painful memories and visions I had were trying to *help me*, by getting me to open up and feel. It worked! We don't need these sorts of emotions to go away, we need to feel them and allow them to move.

Those unwanted emotions prompted such loving and constructive change; how beautiful is that?

If you find yourself mulling over past experiences that hurt you, know that you're not under siege. Your consciousness is simply trying to get your attention. Your mind is showing you where to forgive, where to shift a limiting belief. You have plenty of tools now to do those things! As you progress, you will find that your mind does not constantly replay those awful memories anymore; a true peace will have been made.

Celebrate One Another's Victories

The modern world conditions us to be competitive, judgmental and critical. It encourages fear-based relationships. We don't celebrate one another's triumphs, we envy them. We buy into beliefs about fear, limitation, limited resources and competition. We agree to the rules that there just isn't enough abundance to go around, that we have to claim and protect what's ours.

This is outmoded, old paradigm thinking. It is not life-supportive, it's not helpful to us in any way, at all. In fact, it is a profound misunderstanding that brings much suffering.

It is in your best interest to *celebrate* other people's victories! Make a life practice of celebrating other people's accomplishments, and you will have more in your life worth celebrating.

Remember, we are 100% responsible for *everything* that is in our lives. If a friend calls and says that they met a new wonderful lover, you helped create that love! Their love is your love. Your friend's new relationship is in your line of vision, so to speak. They've chosen to share their joy and love with *you,* so it is a part of *your world*, part of what *you helped create* in your world. If it was not intended as a gift for you, well, they wouldn't be sharing it with you!

Too often, we don't see it that way. When we see other people succeed and blessings rain on them, we may feel jealous, envious, angry, hurt, or fearful. These responses and reactions are letting you know that your perception about the situation is *off,* that you have limiting beliefs that you need to let go of. When we don't feel joy at the success of others, we are not truly understanding the way reality works at all!

So let's get to the heart of the matter, the Truth of the matter:

Your Victories are my Victories.
Your Abundance is my Abundance.
Your Love is my Love.
Your Success is my Success.
On and on it goes!

When I see two people walking down the street hand in hand, smiling at one another, sharing love with one another, I think to myself, "Thank you for that! Their love is my love." I celebrate their love with them. It makes the world more beautiful for me, and that makes me feel good inside.

If something makes you feel good and is not harming anyone then it is *medicine* for you! As I go about my day, everything I lay my eyes upon, I know I helped to create. When I run into people out in the world, I choose to celebrate their successes and victories as my own. This practice raises my vibration, opens me to all of the blessings available, and helps me to manifest those successes in my own life. This is so simple. Feel how much lighter this perspective is!

When we choose to love, support and cherish one another for doing well, we open ourselves to blessings and good fortune finds us. When we choose to be jealous and envious at someone else's success, we shut down the flow of blessings that could come into our life. The envy and jealousy come from a belief in fear-based realities, realities that are out and out lies! These beliefs and choices do not feel good inside us.

So make a commitment to yourself now: cultivate a habit of celebrating other people's victories and you will soon see that your own life is blessed beyond measure.

Acts of Kindness

Performing random acts of kindness is an easy way to spread more love and light and shift your vibration. When we have loving thoughts, when we speak loving words, when we take loving actions, a windfall of Grace is bestowed upon us. The Universe blesses us in return for our blessings of others.

To get guidance on how to perform acts of kindness, consciously and intentionally ask yourself, "How can I bring more love, light and blessings to this world? How can I serve?" Listen for the answers, let the Universe lead, guide and direct you. Do what feels right in your heart.

The Dalai Lama said *"Once you shift your focus from yourself to others and extend your concern to others, this will have the immediate effect of opening up your life and helping you to reach out. The practice of cultivating altruism has a beneficial effect not only from a religious point of view but also from a mundane point of view; not only for long-term spiritual development but even in terms of immediate rewards."* Right on!

This quote was e-mailed to me by a dear friend after I spoke with her about writing this chapter. We talked about my insights and experiences with random acts of kindness, and afterward, she received the quote in an e-mail. She saw the connection and forwarded it to me, and now I'm able to share this quote with you. This is Divine Grace in action! See how reality works? How everything really does line up for the mutual benefit and highest good of all?

I have found that if I am in a funky, bad mood that random acts of kindness can quickly snap me out of it. We are hard wired to feel good when we enlighten, love and bless those around us.

Here are some of favorite "random acts" that lift my mood and brighten someone else's day:

- Put extra money in a parking meter so the next person doesn't have to

- Hold the door for someone at the store

- Let someone cut in line in front of me if they look stressed and as though they really need a break

- Pay for the car behind me when I go through the toll booth

- Let someone get in front of me in traffic

- Stop to let a family walk across the street with their children, and wave wildly with a big smile on my face

- Give a great waiter or waitress an over-the-top tip

- Tell someone you love them or writing them a card letting them know all that you love and appreciate about them, brightening their day, just because you can!

What would happen if everyone on the entire planet woke up tomorrow and said, "How can I serve?" or "What can I do today to make someone else's life a little brighter and easier?"

I want you to close your eyes right now, and imagine, see, feel, and allow a world like that. Notice how this makes you *feel*. Makes your heart open doesn't it? It softens you. Soft is good. Be kind and gentle to yourself and others. Be kind to the earth and to the life of the earth. Tread gently.

What is Enlightenment?

Enlightenment is a shift that takes place within you, a shift *to your natural state of being.* You were created to be happy, loving, prosperous and joyful; you were designed to flow and feel emotion effortlessly.

When the life force within you first awakens, life can feel dramatically different and electric, like you've stuck your toe in a light socket, but after you've lived it consistently for a while, it feels rather normal.

The Grace Blessings that you've received will spark this Enlightenment process for you. As it ignites, you'll notice an increased inner peace, less worry and stress. Things that used to bother you simply won't seem to matter anymore. Outer circumstances won't trigger reactions from you as easily, and if they do, you'll get over it quickly. You'll find you have more energy, that creativity flowers, and synchronicities happen more and more often. Old negative patterns, behaviors, programs and limitations fall away without working on them. Anything within you that is not *you* dissolves and dismantles.

You may feel you are observing or witnessing yourself, no longer identifying with your mind. The mind will never stop doing what it does, but it won't have power or control over you; you'll no longer buy into everything the mind tries to tell you is true. You will be aware of feelings and emotions, but they will no longer rule you.

In Enlightenment, you are able to just experience each present-now moment, without feeling the need to fix, change or resist it. Your perceptions of reality shift and change; you'll see and feel things more clearly. You view the world through the eyes of the Divine, seeing the dramatic beauty within everything, full of love and compassion. You feel completely connected to everyone and everything, at One with the Earth, the life of the Earth and all life forms.

This is not a mind concept, it is a *feeling,* and it cannot be faked. Your Enlightenment will fully flower in Divine time, when you are ready. Enjoy the process; there is no finish line to cross. Enlightenment is never ending. You are constantly expanding, evolving, awakening, growing and changing all the time, just as our Creator always is evolving and changing. The Creator expands, grows and evolves through us, as us.

Enlightenment is a flowering of the heart, an experience of deep love for everything and everyone. This opening of the heart is the mark of True Enlightenment. It is an experience of the world being contained within you, while simultaneously the world surrounds you; there is no separation. You feel as though you are everything and nothing, all at once. There really are no words to describe it. Any attempt to explain pales next to the reality.

The Divine has a unique path created in this process just for you, your very own personal enlightenment. Everyone's journey is exclusive to them. You can design your own Enlightenment process any way you wish, so if you want more burning bush experiences, ask for them! All you need to do is let go of control and give it over to the Divine.

Isn't it interesting that we don't trust the Divine to take care of us and our lives? We want to do it "our way", force our own will, struggle and strain. Try to let go of any concepts you may have about what enlightenment is supposed to even look like. Let it unfold authentically for you the way the Creator has designed it to be, as He/She knows best. Let go and enjoy each gift as it comes. Do not become attached to the gifts, just be grateful when you receive one. Savor the experience, then let go and be open to the next one!

Your Feelings are Your Map

Your feelings are your roadmap; they tell you where and how you are vibrating as you move through your life journey. Vibrations radiate from you like a radio tower, manifesting and creating in your reality. Like attracts like, so you will attract similar vibrations, people, events and circumstances to you.

To get information on how your vibrations are currently aligned, look at your life, look at your feelings. What are you attracting? What are you feeling? The Divine gifted you with feelings to give you a clear indicator of what vibrations you are emitting; your feelings are a signal of how close or far you are from your Divine self. Your feelings let you know your vibration.

Your Divine self is always in the highest of vibrations. The closer you are to the Divine, the higher your vibration, and the better you will feel. Being separated from your Divine self and feeling the lower emotions is not wrong or bad, there is no judgment here. But those lower emotions will not get you to where you want to be in life. If you are attracting unwanted people, events and circumstances then you must shift your inner vibration to attract more positives into your life.

If you have goals, dreams, hopes and desires that you aren't sure are coming to fruition, check your vibration, check your feelings. You will know what you are creating through your feelings. When you know what you are radiating and creating, you won't be sideswiped by unexpected manifestations.

If you have veered off course and away from your Divine self, you can get back in alignment at any time, but you have to know where you are first!

If you are radiating lower emotions like fear, anger, hopelessness, apathy, despair, or irritation, you want to make *steady progress*, so that you feel a little better and better, moving your vibration up until you have reached peace and happiness, then on up into joy and bliss.

Don't expect to shoot up the scale from despair to bliss - that may be a bit of a stretch. Not that it isn't possible; I have seen it happen in private sessions! But that sort of sudden change isn't the goal. Just move up the scale with a steady pace, finding solid ground at each level. Take it one step at a time and you won't feel like a pendulum, swinging from lows to highs. You will discover in this unfolding process that your highs will feel higher and your lows will feel higher, too. It's a gradual shift upward.

The goal is to get up into the higher vibrations with your Divine self, in every area of your life. We vibrate at different levels in various areas, so check your feelings for guidance in each part of your life. The higher your vibrations rise, the better you will feel, but only you can know what feels better for you. After all, it's *your* roadmap!

* * *

Practice Not Naming Your Emotions

Try just feeling your emotions, without names or labels, and notice whether it feels good or not. You are given the gift of free will; you get to choose in each and every moment whether to align yourself more closely with your Divine Self or not. Your feelings are your map. Let them guide you in this.

Pay attention to how you feel in different parts of your life. If you can tell how good (or not so good) you feel in any one area, then you will know where you need to raise your vibration in order to get to where you want to be. Your feelings will also tell you if what you are trying to manifest in your life is close or far away. If you feel joyful about it, you know it is coming soon. If you feel fearful or tense, you know you are adding contradictory vibrations and what you are desiring will take longer to arrive. If you pay attention, you will feel anything unwanted coming a mile away, and you can change your course of action before

anything ugly even has time to manifest. There's great power in this
knowledge!

Everything is energy. The lower emotions are slower and denser in
vibration; the higher emotions that your Divine self experiences are free
flowing, lighter and faster. As you feel better and your vibration lifts,
your energy flows unimpeded and you gain power and momentum.

Many people feel negative emotion so consistently that they think that is
normal. It isn't! Your False Self feels fearful and resistant much of the
time because that is its nature. Be soft and easy on your False Self, it is
doing the best it can with the tools it has been given. It is fearful, so even
if something great comes along it is conditioned to go into fear and
resistance. Take a strong intention to feel good, to be in maximum
alignment with your Divine Self; this intention will win out eventually,
no matter how hard your False Self fights it.

* * *

Get Acquainted with Your Feelings

Pay attention to your feelings in a non-judgmental way. Just observe
them. Approaching your emotions from a neutral place, declare "This is
the way I feel, it is what it is."

Your mind will want to know *why* you feel how you feel, but the reasons
don't really matter. Maybe there is no *why,* maybe the feeling just *is.*
Don't question and get into your head, simply feel. Feeling isn't for
figuring out, it is for feeling!

We are conditioned to indulge in stories about how we got to where we
are, whose fault it is, how right we are and how wrong the other is. By
staying in the story you lose power. By telling the stories over and over,
you will keep recreating that same old story. Do yourself a favor now
and drop it, do not indulge it no matter how badly you want to do so.
Please, please *please* love, support and cherish yourself enough to *not*
tell the story.

Find another way to get the story out of you, if you need to. Write the
story in your journal. Tell yourself a more empowering story. Practice

forgiveness with the story. Feel your feelings and allow them to flow on through. Ask the Divine Presence to show you the truth of the situation.

The real Truth has the most power. When you feel powerful you create a more beautiful reality for yourself. Drop the stories, and take your power back now!

Slow and Steady, One Step at a Time

As your emotions rise to a better vibration, celebrate that improvement. We live in a world governed by cause and effect and the Law Of Attraction. What you feel and vibrate creates your current reality; what you focus on is what you will get more of in your life. When you put your attention on feeling even just a little bit better, it gives momentum to higher and lighter emotions, and soon you will be feeling a *lot* better! Celebrate each and every step of victory.

If you are feeling low about a particular part of your life, don't expect to change your vibration completely in just one day. That isn't the goal! The goal is to feel a little bit better today. When you focus on "feeling a little better today", then you will feel a bit better tomorrow. You will naturally climb slowly and steadily. Just put one foot in front of the other, and in even a week's time you will look back and see just how much progress you have made!

Slow and steady is doable, and easy to maintain over time.

If you are feeling a bit better about relationships today, it means more harmonious, peaceful and wonderful relationships will be forming and coming into your life tomorrow.

If you get frustrated, the flow of energy slows down or even reverses, because *manifestation follows energy.* Value feeling good in each present-now moment. Do it for you! Make it a practice.

Throughout the day, give all cares, struggles, worries, issues and dilemmas over to the Divine Presence. Lay it all down at the feet of the Divine. Before you go to bed, take time to get still, be quiet and breathe.

Prostrate, and give over everything difficult and unwanted. Then celebrate the good!

Divine Grace can lift you up and override even the Law Of Attraction. It gives you a huge vibrational boost so you can reclaim your power. As you receive more Grace Blessings, you open and expand so that you are able to allow in more and more good things. I have seen people in private sessions who came in struggling and feeling hopeless. They receive their Grace Blessing, and their vibration rises up - they leave feeling peaceful, hopeful, even inspired! And yet we did not "work" on a thing. It is like jumping realities instantaneously; as your consciousness shifts, so does your reality.

Here is your next Grace Blessing. Please gaze at the artwork for a few minutes. Then close your eyes and rest for twenty minutes or longer. Then simply go about your day. See what you notice. Observe what is different? Notice how your body feels. Notice how your heart feels. Just notice. Be soft. Be gentle. Love yourself free!

The Power is Always Within You!

Sometimes when we feel bad, we start fixing things on the outside. We want other people's behavior to change. We remodel the house. We change jobs. We move, lose weight, get a makeover. We think *changing the outer* will make us happy. But our lasting happiness does not depend on outer circumstances. If you think yours does, watch out! Trying to control, persuade or manipulate outer circumstances and people is a recipe for disaster.

Your outer world will shift when you change your feelings and thoughts about it. *Change the inner and the outer will change.*

Don't try to make large life plans and decisions when you are in a low vibration; wait until you raise your vibration first. Think back over your life. Have you ever made a good decision when you were in a place of fear, anger, irritation or frustration? Probably not! When we take action when we are in a lower vibration it requires more effort. It is not as efficient or effective. For better results, raise your vibration, and *then* take guided action.

Anger as a Gateway to Reclaiming Power

If you are feeling depression, despair, hopelessness, sadness or fear, feeling anger can help you reclaim your power and raise your vibration. Stop for a moment, and feel the answer to this question: Doesn't anger *feel* more powerful than depression or sadness?

Anger is one of the most misunderstood and ridiculed emotions in our culture. Many of us were even punished as little children for feeling angry: no wonder we have such a difficult time with this emotion! But if you are in a lower emotional vibration, feeling anger can and will propel you upward.

Notice that I said feeling, not expressing. Unleashing the anger on the person you are upset with can be quite damaging. Take your anger, blame, revenge thoughts and feelings to the Presence; feel them, but keep them within you.

This is a new way of dealing with things, for most of us. We have been programmed to pick up the phone, call a friend and vent, but that just creates more stories. Feel into the feeling of anger. Speak to the Presence about it, give it over, and you will rise on up the vibrational scale. As you move into a better place, and better-feeling emotions, you'll be able to address the person or situation you're angry with from a place of neutrality, and without blame.

If you do blow up on someone, know that you are only human. As quickly as possible make it right, forgive yourself, move on and do better.

Divine Grace Does Not Override Free Will

Use your free will to stay in the flow of Grace. Consistently focus on what you want, keep your eye on the prize, and keep your vibration in a good place. What you want will come to you.

Sometimes, you may have a contradictory thought about your desire. Say you want a new relationship, but find yourself speaking to others about how all of your relationships have failed. Or maybe you speak about how there aren't many great men that are around your age, and say things like "The good ones are already taken." Those are all contradictory thoughts and vibrations.

How can a great relationship come to you when you are busy in the past, or conjuring up limiting beliefs like "the good ones are already taken"? You cannot. These contradictory thoughts can be the mind's way of showing you a perception or belief that is not life-supportive, a belief that is leading you away from what you actually want.

If this happens, recognize the thought, thank it for showing up, then choose to refocus on what you desire. If the contradictory thought keeps arising, take it to the Presence and ask to be shown the gift that is in it. These sorts of thoughts are most likely your mind showing you where you need to forgive or change your belief or perception about something; stay open to the possibilities.

Don't label these thoughts bad or wrong. Your beliefs vibrate within you, creating your reality; the contradictory feelings about them provide useful information, showing you where you can be more aligned with your truth and reality.

Letting Go of Beliefs that No Longer Serve You

Our bodies, minds and spirits are filled with past experiences. We use those experiences as references for reality and what we believe to be true. But is this a good way to measure the truth of reality? Any belief about an experience you've had holds a vibration of its own; through the Law of Attraction, it is going to attract similar situations and vibrations.

If you believe that you are not lovable, you will attract life circumstances, situations and people to prove that you are correct. Now of course this is false (you are *lovable!*) but if you believe it, it will be true *for you,* in your perceptions. Such beliefs can be really hurtful, and yet we spend our lives manifesting them in our realities.

If you believe "making money is difficult", it will be true for you. If you believe "life is hard", you will manifest that in your experiences. If you believe that "all men are liars and cheaters", you will attract men who lie to you, and on it goes!

Any belief that is not empowering, any belief that does not make you feel good inside *needs to go.* This is as easy as asking the Divine to help you let go of whatever beliefs you hold that are not true. Simply ask for help, stay open, and be willing to create a new belief for yourself.

Create a Give It Over to God List

You do not have to know it all, be it all, do it all. You don't have to figure it all out; it's not your job!

I want you to make a "Give it over to God list." Take out a piece of paper and make an actual, physical list of all the things you would like the Divine *to do for you.* Be especially sure you list anything you have no idea *how* to do.

Give this list over to the Divine, then sit back and watch as the right people, events and circumstances show up to help you. Stay open for inspired thoughts and feelings to emerge, then act from that place of guided action. When the energy is aligned, your actions will be efficient and effortless. Things will get done on their own, by someone else, or you may realize they simply aren't important and let go of them.

I do not act unless I feel inspired, my inner guidance is crystal clear, and I know am in alignment. Of course I complete my daily obligations, but for the rest of my life, things need to feel right for me to move forward. Remember, if you find yourself feeling fearful, confused, or frustrated, raise your vibration and wait before acting, if possible. Things do not always have to be done *right now*! That rushed feeling is usually a some belief or conditioning you've bought into. Wait until it feels right, and then act.

Put the large stuff on the "Give it over to God" list, let go and wait for an urge from within. Go out and live. Let the Divine do the hard stuff; go and do something for you! Rest and recharge. When you come back you will be refreshed, newly inspired and feeling good; feeling good means you are heading in the right direction.

What If This Still Isn't Working?

Sometimes, I hear people say "I'm still not feeling better or getting better results, even with Grace!"

Not one single soul on this planet wishes to be unhappy. If you've received the Blessings and played with the tools in this book, but have not found the liberation you hoped for, do not despair. Remember that your freedom and liberation comes from fully feeling your feelings.

If you're having a tough time, there are things you can do: Give it over to the Presence. Ask for help. Schedule a private session. Attend a weekend seminar or intensive. Get still, silent, go within. These are all ways to move the energy that is keeping you down.

You may also still be consciously or unconsciously resisting *feeling*. Look for these indicators of resistance:

- You are always rushed, always busy, never still

- You settle for less than what you truly desire

- You feel the need to be around people most of the time and fear being alone

- You put up walls and act tough so that no one can get close to you and hurt you

- You avoid intimacy and getting close to people

- You find yourself unable to get things done; you have low energy, slow metabolism, fatigue and heaviness

- You *think* things through, instead of going within and *feeling* things through

- You are often blindsided by people, events and circumstances that you "never felt coming"

- You feel nothing, you feel numb, or you aren't sure how you feel

- You talk a lot and you talk fast

- You act happy, but the "happy" is not genuine, it's not what you are truly feeling inside

Many people do not feel safe feeling their feelings. If you feel this way, it is OK, you are OK. There is nothing (and I mean nothing!) wrong with you. You are not flawed or defective. You simply have not been taught how to feel and what to do with your feelings.

But I have great news for you: once you fully feel into an emotion and it moves on, you will *know through direct experience* that your natural state is happiness. You will know that *feeling* is not a big deal. You will know that feeling unwanted emotion just means *it is moving!* This knowledge will serve you whenever unwanted emotions arise, because then you can say to yourself, "This is only temporary, this feeling won't last forever"! The certain knowledge that unwanted feelings are only temporary can instantly propel you into hope. The darkness can and does lift!

If you are struggling, give anything that feels too big over to the Presence. Ask for help. Ask for assistance with feeling, then allow yourself to feel. If you have a lot of resistance to feeling or you simply don't feel safe feeling, you may need a private session. Moving into Enlightenment means unlearning many things, some of which have taken us way off course. It's ok to ask for help. Be gentle with yourself.

Things are going to get better! Stop and rejoice!

Remove ALL Limitations from Yourself and Be Happy NOW!

What a progressive concept: Be happy now. Choose it.

Everyone seems to have big lists of stuff that we want to have, be and do. Whatever is on this list (a beautiful house, relationship, perfect body, full spiritual awakening) we want it because of a feeling we are after. We believe once we get these things, we will be happier and feel good. Everyone is motivated by feeling; everyone wants to feel good.

So forget the lists! You do not have to wait to be happy until you get the car, the house, the person, the thing. Outer circumstances can and will shift, your happiness does not depend on them. Choose to be happy now! Release yourself from your self-imposed limitations. Have a happy life now, in this present moment, and in the next, and in the next. Get happy first, and then things fall into place. *Remember, energy FIRST, manifestation follows!*

You can use your free will and conscious mind to *choose* happiness. You can choose it again and again for eternity! No matter what is going on "out there," no matter what you have or don't have, things in your life only have the power and control that you give them. You can just choose to be happy.

When you discover that you want something, enjoy the space between the wanting and the having. Savor it like a delicious piece of chocolate. On the spiritual level, things manifest instantaneously. Whatever you want descends into this physical reality as quickly as you become open to receiving it. How do you do that? By raising the vibration around your desire high enough so that you can accept it. Feel great about it. Know with certainty that it is coming. Release your grip so it can come to you!

Take your hands and close your fists right now. If I were to approach you with a bouquet of flowers, how could you accept them if your fists are closed? You cannot. Let go of the grip so that you can receive.

We are always somewhere between the thought of wanting something and attaining it. That's the space we create in. As we dream one dream and it arrives, we dream another and so on; this is our eternal creative nature. You can choose to be happy while you wait for your dreams to manifest, or you can choose to suffer because it is not here yet. Being happy will empower you to create more quickly.

Set yourself free and be happy now!

The Power of Focus

You are the power that creates Universes, and you participated in creating this one.

That's a big thought, isn't it? Think of your focus as a powerful magic wand, one that creates more of whatever you focus upon. What are you creating with that powerful focus? What reality are you creating for yourself?

When you complain, you are waving your magic wand and creating more to complain about. When you focus on what you appreciate, you are creating more things to appreciate. Become aware of where you put your focus. Notice when you're talking about things that are wrong, then stop and change your focus. When you catch yourself thinking about what you don't have, or how horrible anything is, was, or could be, stop and change where you put your attention! You may be "right" about those things, but focusing on them won't make you happy! Remember to ask yourself "Do I want to be right and continue to attract and create more of that unwanted reality, or do I want a beautiful reality and life?"

Choose. The power of where to point your magical wand of focus is entirely up to you. Take a moment now, and imagine what a world it will be when we all know this!

What Is Holding Up Your Happiness?

The False Self has to have everything "perfect" to be happy. It can't be happy if the world leaders are doing this or that. It can't be happy of its body is too fat or too skinny. It can't be happy without a certain amount of funds in the bank, or if something went differently from what it expected, or if other people are doing things "wrong". For the False Self, happiness relies on outer conditions.

For your authentic, Divine self, happiness is unconditional, no matter what is going on. There is a process of mastery involved in this. One day you'll find yourself unconditionally happy and unsinkable no matter what.

Until then, consider these indications that you're caught up in the False Self's concerns:

- Working too hard, forcing your will rather than letting things happen

- Needing to be right and have others be wrong

- Not being impeccable with your word; gossiping and speaking negatively about other people or your life.

- Making assumptions or engaging in any other low vibration behaviors

Choose your thoughts and your feelings carefully, so you keep your vibration up consistently. We have free will and the power of choice, always. When we do not consciously choose, it is easy to let the outer world have too much power over us, our minds, feelings and emotions. Choose to maintain your alignment with your Divine self, and you can let go of the details of your life and how to get what you want. Give the details over to the Divine, put them on your "God will do it for me" list. Go ahead and make intentional decisions when they feel Divinely guided and joyful, but don't fret over the need to decide everything.

Years ago, I chose to stop watching the news, reading the paper, and listening to certain types of music. Now I focus exclusively on things in the world that make me feel good. If it doesn't make me feel good, I do not participate, it's as simple as that. Even though I do not watch the news, I always know what is going on. I am not missing anything except a lot of negativity! You can choose.

Holding back from being the real and authentic you is too great a sacrifice to make. If you are in a stale job, or a relationship that is no longer a vibrational match, you will not move forward on your dreams. If you outgrow your circumstances and make excuses for staying in them, it can cause you to feel low. Just take the first step. Choose to move forward. The journey of a thousand miles begins with putting one foot in front of the other.

If you resist feeling emotion, it can make you feel low as well. To know the inner most workings of your mind, simply look at your life, look at your feelings. All the clues will be there. You may need to forgive yourself or someone else, or there could be a limiting belief that needs to go. Become aware; awareness alone can and does shift much.

When you focus on what hasn't arrived yet in your life, when you keep your attention on what is wrong in your life, you lower your vibration. Choose your focus. Consciously look for things to appreciate, and things will move in the direction you want them to.

Take time to sit and breathe for the sheer joy of it! Move your body with exercise that you enjoy: dance, jog, run, sprint, do yoga, pilates, walk, skip, hike, ride your bike, make love! Body movement helps you to move energy and gets you into your body. Remember to soothe yourself. Speak lovingly to yourself like you would a little child or a close friend.

Your joy will fade when your energy slows down and becomes denser. Now that you are more awake and aware, you have many tools to help you stay in the higher vibrations. Whether you are fully awakened or not, resisting *feeling* or the flow of where Grace is trying to carry you will feel bad.

Happiness Will Begin to Feel Normal

As you continually receive Grace Blessings, the Grace pulls you to your highest and greatest destiny. You will find yourself feeling better and better. You will experience states of bliss, joy and profound peace more regularly. You will stabilize there and it will begin to feel rather normal. This can be confused with feeling that your joy has faded.

If this happens, reflect over the past weeks or months, and you will see how much indeed has changed for you. The higher states of vibration are integrated in your life; it is now just your normal state of being. Your bliss has not faded, just the newness of it has. Relax and know that the journey goes on and on.

As you progress, you will sometimes find yourself on plateaus, but the climb upward and the expansion outward will commence again. Your Divine self will call you forward and you will continue to move higher and become even more open. The expansion is infinite. The more you let go, the more you will open, the higher you can go. That initial jolt into the higher states is a "high" in and of itself. Each time, you will stabilize, and then go even higher.

Your mind may try to evaluate your "progress" and make you feel like this isn't working. Do not buy into that! If you take a moment to reflect and contemplate how far you have come, you will see plenty of evidence to the contrary. The mind has a hard time with miracles and often tries to dismiss them. In workshops and sessions, I have seen people who have had huge burdens of strife, struggle and pain lifted instantaneously from them, but then their mind will either try to ignore it, or explain it away as a freak experience. It is not a freak experience, and it is not imagined. It's just beyond the mind's understanding.

Allow yourself to marvel in the magic and enchantment of your life. Revel in the unlimited possibilities and probabilities that are available, the potential that you have seen and created. Have confidence in it! There is much, much more in store and the best is yet to come.

Every Single Day...

Every single day, participate in things that make your heart sing and bring you joy. Take time to fill your cup. This is your life! This isn't a dress rehearsal, it is your large, grand, exquisite life. What turns you on and excites you? Dancing, sculpting, jewelry making, painting, writing? Maybe it's gardening, exercising, singing, playing with your pets or children, taking long walks in nature. Take time for it! Take time for you! You deserve it.

When your cup is filled to overflowing you will be happy. When you are happy, you light up everyone around you. It sets an excellent example for others, especially for children.

You will be astonished at how much taking time for you helps you to stay open to receive more and more blessings in your life. Do things just because they feel good. Remember if doing something makes you feel good and it is not hurting anyone, it is medicine for your body. Take your medicine: go and do something fun, just because!

Your Next Grace Blessing

To receive the Blessing, please gaze at the artwork for a few minutes. When you feel this is complete, please close your eyes and rest for twenty minutes or longer.

Sleep On It, Dream On It!

Did you know that with Grace, you can solve problems in your sleep? I have been doing dream assignments for ages; they really and truly work. How much easier can it get? When you want change in your life, when you want to achieve a goal, just give it over to Presence before you sleep, and have it be done *for you.*

To do this, make a list in your journal before you retire for the evening, or speak directly to the Divine about what you would like assistance with. The sky is the limit here, think big! While you are sleeping, you are completely open; vast resources, solutions and creative powers are at your disposal.

The Presence is at your service. It is like your own personal secretary who knows all of the resources available, all possible solutions, all of the right people to get the job completed. The Presence knows how to do things with the least effort, and wants you to succeed, be prosperous and be very, very happy. This vast aspect of *you* is always on duty, wanting to fulfill all of your heart's desires, even in your sleep.

Remember, all things come in Divine time. If your desire does not show up immediately, *savor the waiting.* The answers and solutions you seek may not arrive in your dream itself; they often show up later. Be open to them.

The Deliberate Art of Daydreaming

Remember when you were a little child, how you would daydream and use your imagination to its fullest? Do yourself a favor and indulge deliberately in this practice again! Have fun with it; allow yourself to dream! Daydreaming helps the process of manifestation. Use it when you are in the waiting period between the wanting and the having. It speeds things along!

If you've ever done competitive sports, you've probably used visualization to increase performance. Visualization is just deliberate daydreaming.

A friend of mine dated a gold medalist snow boarder. He worked with her consistently on *imagining* how she was going to do the runs, tricks and twirls in the air. It worked incredibly well, obviously. Her performance improved and she got the gold!

A practice of intentional daydreaming is effective, not only for snowboarders or professional athletes, but in our day to day lives as well. It keeps us focused and feels good; feeling good is important!

How Can You Help the People Around You?

Just be *You!*

Love, accept and honor people exactly as they are. Don't try to fix or heal them.

Live by example, and walk your talk. As the old saying goes, actions speak louder than words. If you speak all the right things but your actions contradict them, people will feel you're in-authenticity and turn away. So walk it, walk it, walk it.

You don't need to be perfect. You only need to practice what you are learning. Aren't we all practicing how to be the best, most loving human beings that we possibly can be? We are practicing *now*, with the tools in this book, because we were never taught out in the world.

When people notice how lit up and happy you are becoming, you can tell them about this book and the things that have been helping you. Don't stuff it down people's throats, just offer it gently.

When people are in a much different vibration than you, they sometimes cannot hear you at all. It is like a dog whistle. Human ears are not tuned to that sound, we cannot hear it. If someone is in a much different place than you are, they may have a difficult time relating; you are not tuned to the same things. Keep this in mind. The goal is peace in our lives, not alienating people - being pushy is counterproductive.

As you undergo your unfolding and enlightening process you will affect those around you. You may find that your partners and friends feel the effects of your awakening process, and begin to awaken themselves. We are catalysts for one another.

You may also find that once you are tapped into the Presence within, you no longer crave or desire reading spiritual books or going to spiritual workshops. As your authentic self develops and blooms, questioning ceases; direct knowing and living fully as your authentic self takes over. The days of seeking and suffering can be over if you choose.

You will begin to feel that you are home wherever you are. Your physical body is your temple, you carry it wherever you go, it is your very own personal, sacred space. Other people will recognize this, and be comforted, soothed and lifted in your presence.

Do You Feel Like You're on a Roller Coaster?

Or maybe that you are swinging like a pendulum?

By now, you have received a number of Grace Blessings, and you are exactly where you need to be on this journey. Your vibration is shifting upwards. At this point, some people feel like they are on a really fast ride. It's as if their feelings and emotions are all over the place, swinging from one extreme to another, often without reason.

This is a common part of the Enlightenment process. As long as you allow yourself to feel it all, and let it flow, it won't last long. It will even out eventually. I promise!

Our False Self is so fearful of change that it even fears change that is good for us, change we have been waiting for a long, long time. Again, this is all perfectly fine. That fear is fine. Let it be ok.

Many people get enough energy, light, and information for their awakening just by reading this book. If you want to go deeper, if you want more, this is perfectly alright, too. It is our nature to want to go further and expand. How exciting it is to finally find something that brings lasting results and that works consistently!

Create a "God Box"

I'd like to leave you with one more tool to help you create the life you want: a "God Box"! You'll need a box, of any size or shape you like.

Place it next to your bed, or wherever is convenient. Whenever you have a worry, care, concern, wish or desire, write it down on sheet of paper, and date it. Place it into the "God Box" and know that it is handled! Only write each concern or desire down *once!* Trust that it will be taken care of for you. The Divine will work the magic, once you let it go and give it over.

After a few months, open the box and look at all that the Divine has taken care of *for you!*

Have fun with this! Be creative. Decorate your box if you like - it is magical!

With Love, From Erica Rock

No matter what events, circumstances or situations you are facing, your job is not to fix it. You do not need to know how to resolve things. You do not need to work harder at solving problems. Your job is to receive Grace. To celebrate your own success. To celebrate the success of others. To unfold and align your vibrations with the TRUE You.

Grace opens you, unfolding the True You so that all of the blessings and solutions that you need can come through. You only need to move your mind out of the way, release resistance, and allow Grace to come in. The energy of the Grace Blessings in this book will not dissipate; when you need extra support, gaze at the artwork in this book.

Remember the tools for letting go that you have learned:

- Prostrate. Lay it all down at the feet of the Divine.

- Create and speak "I AM" statements.

- Place your problems and desires on a "God will do it for me" list.

- Make a dream assignment before you go to bed.

- Participate in activities that bring you joy; go live your life and have fun.

- Choose to be happy and feel good no matter what - use your free will!

- Sit, get still, go within and pray. Ask for help.

- Celebrate your success, celebrate the victories of others.
- Consciously direct the flow of Divine energy within you.
- Create a "God Box"
- Feel your feelings, all of them, without judgment or making them wrong.
- Be at peace with what is.

I wish you a joyful, peaceful, prosperous life. Thank you so very much for embarking on this enchanting and exciting journey with me. Awakening is the answer for every issue we face on this planet. You are now part of the solution.

Go live and enjoy your life. Life is for living. Spread your joy unto the world. Practice what you have learned. Be kind, easy and gentle on yourself. Let go and let God.

Love, love, love
Erica Rock

Please accept the Grace Blessing infused in this image. Gaze at the art for a few minutes, then close your eyes and rest for as long as possible! Enjoy!

Appendix: Further Support & Grace Blessings Resources

People from all over the world participate in live Grace Blessing teleconferences; it provides them with a more personal experience and extra guidance. Live courses are always available. We also offer three and five day silent retreats. These are amazing transformational experiences. In them, you are initiated to give Grace Blessings yourself, becoming a permanent field of resonance for this energy. There is lots of support for you on this journey, if you want it! Do what feels right to you, everyone is different.

Please write me to share your experiences and victories, or join our forums. I may not be able to respond directly, as I receive a lot of e-mail, but I want to hear about your success so I can celebrate it! If you are feeling stuck, and have tried everything in this book, but things don't seem to be moving in the direction you'd like them to, schedule a private session.

Be sure to check the website at http://www.ericarock.com often! New resources are being added to assist in this unfolding process. The following are already available:

- The *Mastery of Mind and Emotions* program is must have for anyone on this journey. It offers additional guidance on the most crucial exercises in this book.

- The *Infinite Blessings* music is infused with Intention and Grace Blessings, so you can have the energy and entrain to it whenever you'd like. The longer you are in the energy, the easier it is to hold that high vibration on your own.

- An *Infinite Blessings* book is also available, containing 36 pieces of beautiful artwork that have been infused with Divine Energy for your reflection, contemplation and entrainment to the Divine energies contained within. The accompanying texts are sutras, spiritual messages that bypass the mind and speak to the truth of your heart. They have the power to transform and heal. *Infinite Blessings* is a specialty work of art that is powerful and highly transformative.

- The *Flying on the Wings of Love* audio program is inspired by Howard Wills prayers and includes simplified versions of the prayers along with an additional Grace Blessing and a peacemaking exercise.

- The *8 week Grace Blessing Mastery Course* is held by live teleconference and available through a previous downloadable recording, so you can participate from anywhere in the world. This class is like embarking on your own personal intensive. It is the next best thing to the live retreats, and will greatly accelerate your journey.

More online classes are being developed and will be available shortly. So stay in touch, check in on the website regularly, and celebrate your Blessings!

Additional Resources:
- *Gift of Life Prayers and Affirmations* - www.howardwills.com

- *Ananda Mandala: chakra breathing and clearing meditation* - available on Amazon.com

- *Reality Works: Let it happen* by Chandra Alexander - also available on Amazon.com